Cambridge Elements

Elements in the Philosophy of Immanuel Kant
edited by
Desmond Hogan
Princeton University
Howard Williams
University of Cardiff
Allen Wood
Indiana University

KANT ON MARRIAGE

Charlotte Sabourin
Douglas College

Shaftesbury Road, Cambridge CB2 8EA, United Kingdom

One Liberty Plaza, 20th Floor, New York, NY 10006, USA

477 Williamstown Road, Port Melbourne, VIC 3207, Australia

314–321, 3rd Floor, Plot 3, Splendor Forum, Jasola District Centre, New Delhi – 110025, India

103 Penang Road, #05–06/07, Visioncrest Commercial, Singapore 238467

Cambridge University Press is part of Cambridge University Press & Assessment, a department of the University of Cambridge.

We share the University's mission to contribute to society through the pursuit of education, learning and research at the highest international levels of excellence.

www.cambridge.org
Information on this title: www.cambridge.org/9781009619370
DOI: 10.1017/9781009304559

© Charlotte Sabourin 2025

This publication is in copyright. Subject to statutory exception and to the provisions of relevant collective licensing agreements, no reproduction of any part may take place without the written permission of Cambridge University Press & Assessment.

When citing this work, please include a reference to the DOI 10.1017/9781009304559

First published 2025

A catalogue record for this publication is available from the British Library

ISBN 978-1-009-61937-0 Hardback
ISBN 978-1-009-30454-2 Paperback
ISSN 2397-9461 (online)
ISSN 2514-3824 (print)

Cambridge University Press & Assessment has no responsibility for the persistence or accuracy of URLs for external or third-party internet websites referred to in this publication and does not guarantee that any content on such websites is, or will remain, accurate or appropriate.

Kant on Marriage

Elements in the Philosophy of Immanuel Kant

DOI: 10.1017/9781009304559
First published online: March 2025

Charlotte Sabourin
Douglas College
Author for correspondence: Charlotte Sabourin, sabourinc@douglascollege.ca

Abstract: This Element proposes a new understanding of Kant's account of marriage by examining the context and background conversations that shaped its development and by discussing the conception of equality at its core. Marriage as Kant understands it relies on a certain form of equality between spouses. Yet this conception of equality does not precede marriage, and carries important limitations – one of which being its inaccessibility to a significant proportion of the German population at the time. The protections and rights conferred by marriage were thus not accessible to all. Their shared preoccupation with this issue allows the author to put Kant's thoughts in relation with those of eighteenth-century feminist writers Theodor von Hippel and Marianne Ehrmann. Despite these limitations, the author finds that Kant's conception of marriage is compatible with the achievement of certain egalitarian goals, suggesting that it may be able to improve women's lives in a liberal state.

Keywords: Kant, marriage, women, Hippel, feminism

© Charlotte Sabourin 2025

ISBNs: 9781009619370 (HB), 9781009304542 (PB), 9781009304559 (OC)
ISSNs: 2397-9461 (online), 2514-3824 (print)

Contents

1 Introduction   1

2 Marriage in Eighteenth-Century Germany   6

3 On Those Who Did Not Marry: Kant and the Infanticide Debate   21

4 Kant and the Community of Marriage   34

5 Concluding Remarks   52

   References   55

1 Introduction

Marriage is no longer a marginal preoccupation in Kantian studies. While Kant discusses marriage only sparingly in his works, Kant scholarship has been enriched over the past couple of decades by many innovative critical reflections on his account of marriage. This wave of interest in what used to be a neglected topic would not have been possible without the work of prominent scholars like Barbara Herman, Howard Williams, Allen Wood, or Pauline Kleingeld, who put forward bold interpretations of Kant's ideas and normalized talking about marriage as a topic of interest in Kant's moral and political philosophy.

While talking about Kant and marriage is no longer unusual, it is still radical. Matthew Altman, Elizabeth Brake, Lara Denis, Jordan Pascoe, Martin Sticker, and Helga Varden, along with many other scholars, have proposed groundbreaking interpretations of Kant's account of marriage – some focusing on its emancipatory possibilities, others emphasizing its problematic limitations. Writing this Element would not have been possible without those, and many more, contributions. It is also indebted to the growing body of work engaging with the topic of marriage in early modern philosophy from a feminist perspective.

When I took on this project, I was hoping to put forward a definitive answer as to whether Kant's conception of marriage is conducive to feminist projects or rather incompatible with those. I have instead realized that we might learn something new by framing the question differently: by asking ourselves what feminist authors who fought for women's lives and rights in Kant's day might have had to say about the conception of equality structuring his account of marriage – and the inequalities he leaves unaddressed.[1] There is very little redemption for Kant if we look at his work from a contemporary feminist standpoint. Even the most positive readings of Kant's ideas take the form of critical appropriations. Varden's 2020 monograph *Sex, Love, and Gender: A Kantian Theory*, for instance, starts by identifying and discussing a number of problematic claims made by Kant prior to proposing positive, yet still critical appropriations of his ideas about sex, love, and gender. Varden argues that this work requires moving away from the usual emphasis placed on Kant's conception of freedom and moral ends, focusing instead on his rich conception of human nature and embodiment. Scholars like Huseyinzadegan and Pascoe have also consistently reminded us of the importance of adopting an intersectional

---

[1] In extending the term "feminist" to early modern reflections on the equality of the sexes as well as political demands and actions aimed at improving the situation of women during that time, I follow the direction set by recent scholarship – for a few examples, see O'Neill & Lascano (2019); many of the titles in the Cambridge Element Series on Women in the History of Philosophy; and in my own work, Sabourin 2021b and 2023a.

feminist perspective when engaging with Kant's ideas – using his views on race, gender, class, and labour to shed some light on the exclusions and hierarchies embedded in his thought. They also emphasize both the importance and the inherent difficulty of this task.

I am hoping that turning back to the context and interlocutors that Kant was engaging with might provide us with additional insights into the nature and degree of equality he valued between men and women. Kant's account of marriage in the *Doctrine of Right* is truly innovative when compared to many contemporary ideas and preoccupations he engaged with – and the equality he postulates between spouses represents a significant transformation of the institution of marriage that should not be trivialized. However, Kant did not extend this reflection to gender equality beyond marital life. This extra step might seem too demanding for the time Kant was writing in – but as I will show, others were actively reflecting on that question in Kant's day, thus making it an issue especially worthy of our attention. Stuckenberg famously wrote, "those who expect from Kant broad views respecting woman, must not forget to study his opinions in the light of that day" (Stuckenberg 1882, 184). The idea that Kant was a man of his time has been profusely used to excuse or dismiss his most shocking claims. But despite his aversion for political revolutions, Kant intended to revolutionize metaphysics, epistemology, and moral philosophy: he had no intention of being simply another man of his time. Regarding him as such, and excusing his faults on these grounds, would be doing justice neither to his ambitions, nor to his time. Without attempting to excuse Kant in doing so, I believe there is an interest in paying closer attention to debates he would have been familiar with. While eighteenth-century German authors did not have access to the conceptual resources developed by Kimberlé Crenshaw on intersectionality, for instance, they presumably did have access to Theodor von Hippel's reflections on the status of women, or to Anton Wilhelm Amo's dissertation on the rights of Moors in Europe. Kant's many thoughts on marriage – some conservative, some groundbreaking – were undoubtedly influenced by the authors he read or heard of. By shedding light on the debates he engaged in, some of which revolved around genuinely feminist preoccupations, I am hoping to propose a new understanding of how innovative his account of marriage was – and also to do justice to the critical conversations that already took place around marriage then. Despite his lack of interest (to say the least) in the status of women, Kant makes unusually clear, in his account of marriage, that spouses shall be equal in the possessions, both material and immaterial, that they share. He also demonstrates a perhaps surprisingly acute awareness of the inequalities faced by women who were unable to enter marriage in his discussion of the legal sanctions imposed for infanticide. But since his views on spousal equality are motivated by their role within his account of marriage and sexuality rather than by a more robust conception of gender equality preceding marriage, he does not consistently address the broader causes of the inequalities he notices between men and women. Kant's original views on spousal equality, along with their blind spots, will be at the forefront of my investigation, divided into three main sections.

In eighteenth-century Europe, marriage gained increasing attention from two important groups of people that will be especially interesting for us to consider here. First, marriage was a topic of interest to middle- and upper-class women writing from a feminist perspective. Treatises and other forms of writings on marriage were allowing these women to share their reflections on the role of marriage as a social institution of direct concern to them, on the inequality and subordination underlying that institution, and on the various conceptions of love, femininity, and sexual difference involved in marriage. While some men have also authored analyses of marriage as a social and political phenomenon, women were major contributors to these discussions. While their exclusion from canonical narratives in the history of philosophy may give the impression that marriage was not an important issue at the time, it has since then become a topic of growing interest for contemporary scholars eager to properly capture the diversity of early modern philosophy.[2] Second, marriage was also a popular topic amongst scholars interested in natural law and the organization of society, due to its prominent role in codifying and regulating sexual interactions. Pufendorf, for instance, describes marriage as constitutive of the state (Donahue 2016, 50). Marriage was construed as a "key institution ... mediating between individual desire and public interest" or even as a "model of civil society" in itself (Hull 1996, 294). Jurists were thus keen to reflect on the meaning and legal implications of marriage. For instance, should the purpose of marriage be limited to procreation, or be extended to the happiness of the spouses? Should parental consent be required for one to marry, or can the spouses' mutual consent prevail? Should marriage be construed as a sacrament of the Church or as a secular matter? Are celibacy, fornication, and polygamy permissible? These legalistic discussions of marriage typically involved different interlocutors than the feminist discussions of marriage, and their underlying motivations were quite different too. There is nevertheless some overlap between the two discussions: for obvious reasons, women were keen to identify and discuss their own rights and protections in marriage. My first section will discuss Kant's involvement with both groups, with a special

---

[2] The twenty-first century has been marked by a growing interest in investigating marriage from a feminist perspective in early modern works. See for instance Broad 2014; Emmett 2022; Forbes 2019.

focus on the different meanings and limitations ascribed to the notion of equality within marriage. It was not uncommon for jurists to describe marriage as a union of equals: Achenwall, for instance, insists on the natural equality of the spouses. But as we will see, this egalitarian assumption often paved the way for cumbersome arguments intending to justify the legal authority and superiority of the husband over the wife despite their natural equality and typically did not go as far as to suggest an equality of possessions as Kant does. Eighteenth-century feminist authors, on the other hand, were more eager to question the arbitrary nature of the authority of the husband over the wife – often grounding their arguments in broader criticisms of the subordination of women in society. Theodor von Hippel, for instance, sees the reform of marriage as a necessary consequence of his stronger conception of the natural equality between men and women. Instead of trying to reconcile marriage with a shallow conception of natural equality, Hippel demonstrates that society must undergo important changes (the reform of marriage being only one of them) to properly account for the fact that men and women are radically equal. While Kant did not directly engage in public conversations with this second group of authors, his personal connection with Hippel makes it especially relevant to see how their different conceptions of marriage interact – and where Kant's falls short. Insights from Marianne Ehrmann and Emilie von Berlepsch will also contribute to giving a better sense of the many feminist reflections on equality that emerged in Kant's day.

The feminist and legal discussions surrounding marriage also reveal an acute awareness of the political power carried by that institution in a context marked by women's inequality. From conferring rights and privileges to one spouse over another to making possible various political alliances, the authority and powers conveyed by marriage made no doubt to Kant and his contemporaries. While negotiating those powers was very important to the women who could marry, they were also aware that important rights and privileges were denied to those who could not enter marriage for reasons related to class, status, or race. The importance of these inequalities between men and women, but also amongst women, justifies turning next to a case of crime and punishment that disproportionately affected working-class women: infanticide and infanticide trials. Women who were unable to enter marriage, as was the case of many working-class women in eighteenth-century Germany, were facing more severe punishments than married women over the suspicious death of a child. The fate of many vulnerable women facing serious charges for crimes that they sometimes were not guilty of, or sometimes had committed in dire, extenuating circumstances, aroused passions. Despite its dark undertones, this feminist preoccupation with infanticide is not new: Adrienne Rich has dedicated part of her monograph on motherhood to that topic,[3] and it is also well represented in the work of historians interested in gender and sexuality like Isabel Hull. Kant, perhaps surprisingly, also took an interest in infanticide trials. Even more surprisingly, we find him wondering if condemned women should be exempt from capital punishment. Despite his negative answer to that question – for Kant, anyone found guilty of murder must receive capital punishment – I find his answer more compassionate than it is sometimes taken to be, and his thoughts reveal, at the very least, a preoccupation with a topic that was also of interest to feminist writers, thus extending the conversation on gender inequality started in the previous section. But Kant leaves the underlying causes of his concerns ultimately unaddressed, whereas authors like Ehrmann and Hippel – who in many ways anticipate Rich's contemporary analysis of the issue – make it clear that the broader circumstances responsible for infanticides must be addressed to prevent the unjust punishment of vulnerable women.

My last section then circles back to Kant's account of marriage in order to investigate the egalitarian possibilities it offers and to overcome some of its limitations. I argue that if we take seriously the equality of the spouses Kant describes and cares about, we must find a way to incorporate this equality into a more formal conception of gender equality that reaches beyond marriage – otherwise, Kant's argument is bound to remain ineffective. I thus bring Kant one step closer to the reforms proposed by Hippel by suggesting that his account of marriage gives us every reason to argue for the equal civil status of men and women in society. I start by further investigating Kant's reasons for making marriage the solution to the problem raised by sex. As is known, Kant sees sexual desire as causing the objectification of oneself and of one's sexual partner, but marriage somehow resolves that problem. Through marriage, the spouses acquire each other, and in doing so they also acquire themselves back. For that reason, that process ought to be reciprocal and egalitarian. Kant also notes that this mutual possession of the spouses must extend to their material possessions for the arrangement to be truly equal and reciprocal. The egalitarian powers that Kant attributes to marriage lead me to take his reasoning one step further, arguing that for these principles to be fully effective, the informal equality it commands between spouses must be formalized by way of their civil status. This reform would ensure that all men and women are granted active citizenship, thereby getting rid of a significant inequality between spouses. I support this claim by drawing on his criticism of the inegalitarian grounds of morganatic marriages – an unconventional type of marriage in which

---

[3] I would like to thank Alice Everly for bringing this reference to my attention and for discussing it with me.

the possessions and titles of one spouse are not extended to the other, which for Kant compromises the very essence of marriage. Kant's concern is right and should be taken seriously. This is why I believe that the significant imbalance in power created by unequal civil status must be addressed by putting forward a more robust conception of gender equality – so that we can properly do justice to the spousal equality that he cared about as well as to broader feminist concerns. My intention is not to suggest that marriage is the path we must follow to improve women's lives – the many exclusions built in marriage have long disproven this – but rather to take seriously an institution that Kant rightly viewed as central to society and right, to assess its role in understanding the importance of a significant commitment to gender equality, and to emphasize the relevance of these questions to the lives of women in Kant's day.

2 Marriage in Eighteenth-Century Germany

The institution of marriage received considerable attention in Kant's day from a wide range of writers interested in different perspectives. While jurists were eager to legislate on and to reform marriage because of the importance it held in German society, feminist writers were equally eager to weigh in, criticize, and transform marriage for its impacts on women's lives. This section argues that Kant's engagement with the institution of marriage must be understood against this twofold background to make sense of the ways in which his own conception of marriage may be described as egalitarian. Kant's complex view of spousal equality, which implies an equality of possessions (both material and immaterial) and of status within the household, is shaped by the preoccupations of jurists of his time. And while Kant engages with some of their concerns, he also departs from common ideas regarding, for instance, the role of procreation in marriage, or the sexual subordination of the wife to the husband. But Kant's conception of spousal equality does not explicitly extend to other aspects of marital life or to civil society beyond the household – thus overlooking the concerns of feminist writers of his time. Mapping Kant's conception of spousal equality, with its innovative aspects and limitations, benefits from engaging with both types of sources.

Kant's account of marriage is undoubtedly more directly influenced by politico-legal accounts of marriage than by early feminist reflections on marriage. The overview of key proposals on marriage put forward by jurists like Samuel Pufendorf, Christian Wolff, Gottfried Achenwall, and Johann Heinrich Gottlob von Justi, all of whom Kant was familiar with, is thus especially helpful in situating Kant's own concerns and reflections. But early feminist accounts of marriage also constitute an important contextual background in understanding

Kant's views. Since we know he was familiar with (at least) Theodor von Hippel's ideas on the matter,[4] it seems reasonable to infer that Kant's reflections on marriage and on the ways in which spouses may or may not be equal to each other were not completely oblivious to these developments. While he decided against addressing feminist issues in his own proposals, a complete reflection on Kant's account of marriage should consider the background he would have had (or perhaps should have had) in mind when engaging in these conversations. This allows for a proper comparison between Kant's original, but narrow conception of the equality required between spouses and more robust conceptions of gender equality like Hippel's.

To further emphasize the importance of marriage for eighteenth-century German Aufklärers, it is worth noting that Kant's famous 1784 essay "What Is Enlightenment?," along with Moses Mendelssohn's, was sparked by the 1783 debate on the legal status of marriage in the *Berlinische Monatsschrift* between Johann Erich Biester and Johann Friedrich Zöllner: should marriage celebrations remain the prerogative of the Church or should the State become in charge of celebrating civil marriages? In 1783, Biester published a "Proposal for the clergy not to be involved in performing marriages anymore." Interestingly, Biester does not argue for the complete secularization of marriage, but rather that religious celebrations should stop being the prerogative of the clergy. Instead, in continuity with Enlightenment ideals, a form of spiritual religion should be built directly into civil procedures (Schmidt 1989, 271).[5]

Biester's piece sparked some controversy, starting with Zöllner's passionate response, "Is it advisable to stop sanctioning marriage through religion?" in which he worries about a sacred institution like marriage, and religion and morality in general, being compromised under the name of the Enlightenment. In a footnote, he shares the question that inspired Kant and Mendelssohn's essays:

> What is enlightenment? This question, which is almost as important as what is truth, should indeed be answered before one begins enlightening! And still I have never found it answered! (cited in Schmidt 1989, 272)

---

[4] Beyond their friendship, since Hippel's major works were published anonymously and that he was, to some extent, influenced by Kant's ideas, there were rumors as to whether Kant might secretly be the author of some of Hippel's works. Kant had to publish a disclaimer in the *Allgemeine literarische Anzeiger* in December 1796 ("Explanation regarding von Hippel's authorship") to make clear that he had not contributed to Hippel's works: "I am not the author of those works, neither alone, nor together with him" (12:360). In this disclaimer, Kant also states that Hippel did not plagiarize his works in any way.

[5] While Biester's ideal of spiritually-informed civil marriages did not become a reality, Prussia did eventually adopt a secularized form of marriage in 1874 (Donahue 2016, 39).

While neither Kant's nor Mendelssohn's essay takes a definitive stance on the status of marriage, they are nevertheless informed by the disagreement between Biester and Zöllner, which exemplifies the importance of a question like marriage for scholars and intellectuals in eighteenth-century Germany.[6] Kant himself, in discussing the distinction between private and public uses of reason, insists on the importance for the clergyman to be able to make public use of his reason, and, perhaps to weigh in on Biester and Zöllner's debate, suggests that it should be possible to propose and publicly discuss possible improvements to a religious organization. Moreover, warns Kant, agreeing to something like a "permanent religious constitution that is to be publicly called into question by no one" is "simply impermissible" (WIE 8: 39). It thus seems like Kant's enlightenment, without going as far as to endorse Biester's reform of marriage over Zöllner's concerns, is supportive of the public nature of their interventions.[7]

Aside from the debate on enlightenment in the *Berlinische Monatsschrift*, marriage was a prominent topic for jurists to weigh in. In the wake of the Reformation, marriage in Germany underwent multiple legal reforms from the sixteenth through the eighteenth century.[8] I will now turn to two core features of marriage that were subject to disagreement amongst jurists and that are especially helpful in contextualizing Kant's account of marriage: the purpose of marriage and the (in)equality amongst spouses it entails. While Kant, unlike many of his peers, rejects procreation as the main purpose of marriage, he nevertheless views marriage as a necessary form of regulation of sexuality. This key role, in turn, motivates his preoccupation with the egalitarian nature of marriage.

In the *Doctrine of Right*, Kant points to the necessity of certain juridical institutions to help us enforce our duties towards others whenever we are at risk of harming them. Marriage is one of those institutions: it is intended to play the role of moral safeguard by providing the only acceptable framework in which sexuality can take place. Kant understands marriage as a "sexual union in accordance with principle [rather than with mere animal nature]"; that is, "the union of two persons of different sexes for lifelong possession of each other's sexual attributes" (MM 6: 277). This core definition leaves out procreation,

---

[6] Schmidt (1989, 271 sq.) and Fleischacker (2013, 11–12) also note the importance of the debates held within the *Mittwochsgesellschaft*, a secret society focused on the Enlightenment, in shaping the context in which Mendelssohn and Kant's essays were published.

[7] As opposed to the discussions of the *Mittwochsgesellschaft*, which were intended to remain secret in nature. Piché (2012) provides an in-depth analysis of Kant's reservations towards secret societies in philosophy.

[8] Donahue notes that many of the changes in marriage law that took place in Protestant countries at the time were similarly and simultaneously implemented in Catholic countries, thereby suggesting that those changes were only partly due to the Reformers' religious views (2016, 41).

which may come across as surprising.⁹ While Kant frequently reminds his readers of the importance of procreation as a natural end of the human species,¹⁰ he also avoids identifying it as the sole or most important purpose of marriage. The preservation of the human species may be the natural end of our sex drive,¹¹ and marriage may be intended to provide an ethical framework for sexuality, but that does not entail that procreation is an end that we ought to set for ourselves in getting married, nor the only end that we can set for our marriage. As extensively shown by Denis, nature's ends should not necessarily guide rational beings, and they cannot prescribe duties independently of the categorical imperative. While moral duties should not conflict with natural ends, the extent to which moral duties must take these natural ends into consideration remains open to interpretation (Denis 1999, 235). One could, for instance, get married for a combination of purposes: engaging in sexual acts intended to fulfill the natural end of procreation, and, at the same time, contributing to the happiness of the couple. One can also wonder to what extent human beings should be held individually responsible for fulfilling an end of nature that is extended to the whole species: the preservation of the species cannot be secured, nor defeated, through the actions of individuals on their own.¹² If celibacy is permissible (and Kant, unlike some of his contemporaries, thought it was), one should infer that it is acceptable for certain individuals not to be contributing to the preservation of the species. Kant thus explicitly criticizes the assumption according to which marriage should be dedicated to procreation in the *Doctrine of Right*:

> The end of begetting and bringing up children may be an end of nature, for which it implanted the inclinations of the sexes for each other; but it is not *requisite* for human beings who marry to make this their end in order for their

---

⁹ Wood notes that Kant breaks with tradition by rejecting procreation as the end of marriage (1999, 257).

¹⁰ In the *Metaphysics of Morals* (MM 6: 277; MM 6: 424, 426), but also in his lectures on ethics, for example, L-Eth Vigilantius 27: 639; L-Eth Herder 27: 48; ...

¹¹ Denis notes that Kant does not go as far as to claim that procreation is the *only* natural end of our sexual inclination either: He also, for instance, hints at how our sexual inclinations are "ennobling man" and "beautifying woman" in the *Observations* (93) (cited in Denis 1999, 245n17).

¹² Similarly, the progression of humanity towards enlightenment, which Kant also construes as a purpose of nature (*UNH* 8: 19), is understood as a collective endeavour that takes place over several generations and that does not require all individuals to equally contribute towards that goal. This insight has been used to shed some light on the unequal contributions to enlightenment that Kant expects from different groups of people. For instance, Piché (2015) argues that Kant's conception of enlightenment does not apply to members of society who are uneducated in the same way than to those who have benefitted from a formal education – the latter being in a position to make a public use of their reason as scholars, but not the former. I have also shown in Sabourin (2021a) that women are not expected to contribute to the public use of reason otherwise associated with enlightenment in *What is Enlightenment?* – an argument that can be extended to other marginalized groups in eighteenth-century Germany.

> union to be compatible with rights, for otherwise marriage would be dissolved when procreation ceases. (MM 6: 277)

While Kant is not promoting sexual fulfillment at the expense of procreation, he does want to make sure that sex acts that are driven by pleasure rather than procreation within the context of marriage are still considered morally permissible, or lawful. This is why Kant grants that procreation (by which he refers not only to the production of children, but also to their upbringing) may well be an end of nature, but that it need not be an end that individuals set themselves when getting married. Otherwise, as he notes, marriage would be dissolved whenever a couple is not able to procreate anymore. However, as noted by Varden, marriage, for Kant, should always at least be in theory *compatible* with procreation (Varden 2020, 118, 121): his account remains heteronormative in that sense.

Kant's account of the purpose of marriage and the role of procreation thus departs from the main options put forward by jurists whose work he would have been familiar with. Achenwall, for instance, defines marriage as follows in the *Ius naturae* – the textbook that Kant used for his lectures on natural law: "A society of a man and a woman, entered upon to produce and bring up offspring (children), is called marriage (matrimony, conjugal society)" (Achenwall, 2021, Natural Law II, §42 [122]).

Achenwall's stance is unambiguous: procreation is the sole purpose of marriage. He further adds that if a man and a woman enter a union for any other reason, that union cannot be regarded as marriage. Pufendorf, Wolff, and Justi (amongst others) similarly identify procreation as the main purpose of marriage. But despite its popularity, this view was not universally embraced in Kant's day. Christian Thomasius, for instance, develops a surprisingly sex-positive account of marriage, emphasizing the importance of sex towards the happiness of both spouses (not just for procreative purposes), and explicitly identifying the happiness of the spouses as a fundamental purpose of marriage alongside procreation (Thomasius, *Von der Kunst vernünftig und tugendhaft zu lieben*, part 4, par. 33, p. 171; cited in Hull 1996, 163). While Thomasius' account is especially remarkable in emphasizing the positive contribution of marital sex to love and, in doing so, moves away from his contemporaries' narrow focus on procreation, these accounts all share a fundamental preoccupation: that of regulating men and women's sex drive through marriage. Channelling that sex drive into procreation was the most common way of doing so. But identifying sex as a positive factor contributing to the happiness of spouses within the boundaries of marriage was also a way of restricting sex to marriage, and of ascribing a definite purpose to sex in conjugal life.

To be sure, Thomasius' positive account of the role of sexuality within marriage avoids pitfalls that more severe accounts were bound to encounter regarding the permissibility of certain sexual acts. If the purpose of marriage is procreation, as argued by Pufendorf, Wolff, Justi, or Achenwall, what should we make of marital sex that is not aimed at procreation? While this question was not a problem for Thomasius, jurists who were committed to procreation being the main and possibly only purpose of marriage had to address several practical issues – whether it is permissible to have sex while being pregnant, for instance, or when conception is no longer possible. Kant, by rejecting the exclusive orientation of marriage towards procreation, avoids this problem – "for otherwise marriage would be dissolved when procreation ceases" (MM 6: 277). He goes as far as to acknowledge the possibility that people may marry with the explicit purpose of experiencing "the pleasure of using each other's sexual attributes" (MM 6: 278), a hypothesis that corroborates, for him, the importance of guaranteeing the equality of the partners beyond sexuality. In permitting, rather than prohibiting, the pursuit of sexual pleasure in marriage, Kant thus shows some relative open-mindedness: this feature of his account of marriage contrasts with the stance of more pleasure-denying jurists (to borrow Hull's expression) like Wolff, who prohibits any sex acts that cannot result in procreation, including, for instance, during pregnancy (Hull 1996, 180). It is of course possible that by softening the requirement to embrace procreation as an individual end, Kant may also have been trying to vindicate his own celibate lifestyle. Some of his contemporaries had been stressing the tension between celibacy and procreation in order to show that a celibate lifestyle conflicts with the preservation of the species. In that stricter perspective, getting married (when one can) would thus be a duty.

Achenwall also has a significantly harsher stance than Kant's regarding sex acts motivated by pleasure rather than procreation within marriage:

> Since producing offspring and raising it once it has been produced cannot but be reckoned among *God's goals*, all intercourse that is contrary to these goals and therefore all sex outside marriage, indeed all use of the genitals for the sake of mere pleasure, in one word: all *straying lust*, goes against the natural divine law. (Achenwall, 2021, Natural Law II, §42 [122])

Achenwall thus leaves very little room for pleasure-motivated sex, even within the boundaries of marriage: any use of the genitals for the sake of mere pleasure, as he says (presumably hinting at masturbating), conflicts with natural law.

The heavy focus on the role of procreation within marriage is also helpful in highlighting the significant bias against homosexuality and same-sex marriage in Kant's day. Interestingly, while homosexuality was about to become an important topic in nineteenth-century discussions of sexuality, it remained mostly underdiscussed throughout the Enlightenment. Hull notes that it does not seem to "fit the social concerns of the late Enlightenment. One might say that the practitioners of late-eighteenth-century civil society were preoccupied with laying down the principles of 'normality'" rather than with further discussing what was perceived as deviance (Hull 1996, 258)[13] – which obviously does not mean that they were tolerant about it. When Kant and his contemporaries mention homosexuality, they are generally keen to regard it as an unnatural form of sexuality (and sometimes also to discuss the punishment that should be associated with it). Same-sex relationships are thus reduced to their sexual dimension, and very rarely discussed beyond the impermissibility of that sexuality.[14]

Indeed, for Kant, sexual union may take a natural form (by which procreation is possible) or an unnatural form (by which procreation is not possible). He includes under the latter homosexuality and bestiality, and claims that both are transgressions of principles that "do wrong to humanity in our own person." In contrast, marriage is defined as a sexual union in accordance with principle (MM 6: 277). For that reason, the idea of same-sex marriage seems to represent a contradiction in terms, since it relies on a sexuality deemed unnatural. However, recent Kant scholarship has demonstrated that his dismissal of same-sex marriage on these grounds is inconsistent. Altman's 2010 article, now a canonical reference on the matter, notes that Kant allows for sex within marriage that does not aim at the natural end of reproduction – thus weakening his argument against homosexual sex (Altman 2010, 326). This problem also grounds Sticker's more recent argument regarding the compatibility of same-sex marriage with Kantian philosophy: "[homosexuality] . . . would not thwart the natural end of procreation – it simply does not advance it" (Sticker 2020, 446).[15] In that sense, Kant's relative flexibility regarding the role of the natural end of procreation in marriage may be disserving his objection to same-sex

---

[13] It may also be the case that Enlighteners were interested in discussing certain types of "deviance" over others: Polygamy, for instance, is a topic that seems to have generated more extensive discussion, and perhaps more fascination, than homosexuality in Kant's day.

[14] Most discussions of homosexuality are also further biased in that they remain overly focused on male homosexuality and on the prohibition of sodomy – thus contributing to lesbian erasure. When defining *crimina carnis contra naturam* (a category later taken up in the *Doctrine of Right*) in the Collins lectures on ethics, Kant indicates that he also includes women in his prohibition of homosexuality, "i.e., when a woman satisfies her impulse on a woman, or a man on a man" (L-Eth Collins 27: 391). But even these brief mentions remain infrequent in legal works. While they were not often depicted in a positive light, lesbian relationships were discussed somewhat more frequently in literary works of the same period – Denis Diderot's *La Religieuse* being a famous example.

[15] Pascoe, while acknowledging the transformative possibilities offered by Kant's account of marriage, importantly remarks that it would not do well as a *universal estate* due to its inability

marriage. Wolff, in prohibiting any sex that is not directed towards procreation, offers a different argument against homosexuality: he portrays homosexual sex as a choice made by some men to satisfy their sex drive without having to negotiate the challenges of marriage – thus, as a form of avoidance of responsibility (*Vernünfftige Gedancken von dem gesellschaftlichen Leben der Menschen* 16, cited in Hull 1996, 176).

As exemplified by Wolff's argument, Kant's sources also understand marriage in unquestioned heteronormative terms. We have seen that Achenwall defines marriage as "a society of a man and a woman, entered upon to produce and bring up offspring" (Achenwall, 2021, Natural Law II, §42 [122]). Kant's contemporaries also take up this heteronormativity, even the most progressive: while Hippel, for instance, does not restrict marriage and sexuality to procreation, he still grounds marriage in the natural complementarity between men and women. Nothing in their works seems to indicate an awareness of same-sex relationships, despite their unquestionable existence. Justi is a notable exception: in claiming that sexual satisfaction is not compatible with marriage, he argues that "otherwise it would nonsensically follow that a true marriage could occur between man and man and woman and woman. There can after all be no doubt that persons of a single sex can give one another mutual aid and be in a permanent community of life together." (*Rechtliche Abhandlung* 31, cited in Hull 1996, 181). While Justi's conclusion is unfortunate, his explicit acknowledgement of the existence of same-sex unions at least demonstrates some degree of awareness that homosexuality carries the possibility of meaningful relationships.

While Kant's account offers a different perspective on the roles of procreation and sexual pleasure in marriage, it nevertheless shares an important similarity with the views of Pufendorf, Wolff, Justi, or Achenwall: it grants marriage a form of control over sexuality by allowing it to set criteria for acceptable and unacceptable sexualities (as shown by the examples of homosexuality and non-marital sex). So while Kant rejects the claim according to which procreation is the (main or only) purpose of marriage, he does share in the assumption that marriage provides the only acceptable framework for sex – and that marriage should be structured accordingly. For that reason, Kant's account of marriage carries some egalitarian implications, which have been extensively investigated, praised, and criticized.[16] The most salient of these implications is

---

to support the decriminalization of the sexual practices of those who are denied the right to marry (Pascoe 2018, 17).

[16] While most contemporary commentators are understandably critical of Kant's remarks on women, it is widely agreed that his conception of marriage postulates a relative equality of the

that in order for sex to take place in an ethical – lawful – manner, Kant argues that spouses must possess each other in a complete and equal manner:

> [...] the relation of the partners in a marriage is a relation of *equality* of possession, equality both in their possession of each other as persons (hence only in *monogamy*, since in polygamy the person who surrenders herself gains only a part of the man who gets her completely, and therefore makes herself into a mere thing), and also equality in their possession of material goods. (MM 6: 278)

This equality is especially important with respect to marital sex. Kant conceives of sex as an intrinsically objectifying act by which one is turning themselves, as well as their sexual partner, into a thing. The only way to overcome this form of objectification consists in transforming it into a perfectly equal and reciprocal form of possession, where spouses mutually possess one another and thereby gain their own person back. Kant's argument is complex and requires further analysis, which will be completed in the last section of this volume. Yet it clearly postulates a form of equality that extends beyond sexuality to other aspects of the spouses' lives, in particular to material possessions: what belongs to one must also belong to the other. These specifics make his conception of spousal equality difficult to categorize. It is in some ways formal (since it relies on the equality of the spouses as persons) and in some ways material (since it involves the sharing of possessions, including material ones). But the equality put forward by Kant is not entirely satisfying on the formal level either (as the spouses do not necessarily enjoy equal civil status), nor on the material level (as it does not address how the spouses will be able to freely enjoy their mutual possessions, for instance). This complex notion of equality also stands in contrast to some of Kant's dismissive claims on women, and non-European women of colour in particular – and these tensions ultimately lead me to regard women's inferior legal status as incompatible with Kant's egalitarian ambitions for marriage. For Kant, women are bound to be passive citizens, that is second-class citizens who are deemed immature from a civil standpoint[17]: they do not have the right to vote, for instance, and they are placed under the legal tutelage

---

spouses (cf. Herman 1993; Hull 1996; Papadaki 2010; Varden 2020; etc.) Disagreements occur with respect to the extent and significance of this equality. Kleingeld (2019) and Pascoe (2022) both express important criticisms of Kant's account of marriage from intersectional perspectives – emphasizing respectively that its egalitarian aspect does not extend to non-European women, women of colour, slaves, or servants within a European household (Kleingeld 2019, 7–10), and that his account of women is limited to wives and as such does not engage with the question of women servants or with intersections of gender and race within the household (Pascoe 2022, 47 sq.).

[17] I argue elsewhere that it is this very specific, civil notion of immaturity that prevents women from actively participating in Kant's conception of enlightenment. (Sabourin 2021a).

of their husband or father. I will argue in Section 4 that this difference in civil status compromises the egalitarianism that Kant tries to achieve and that women must obtain an equal status for Kant's conception of marriage to at least accomplish what he intended. While Kant's preoccupation with equality carries important limitations that must be addressed, it nevertheless remains a core feature of his account of marriage. It is also worth noting that this preoccupation was widely shared in his day, though to varying degrees.

Relevant to this perhaps surprisingly widespread preoccupation with equality is the fact that eighteenth-century accounts of marriage came with their fair share of restrictions as to who was allowed to enter marriage in the first place. Some of these restrictions were contextual – like, for instance, the ban on marriage for ordinary soldiers in seventeenth-century Baden-Baden in order to reduce pension costs and other requests (Hull 1996, 109), or the increase in the age requirement for servants to get married in Bavaria around the same period, intended as a countermeasure to labour shortages in the countryside (Wunder 2016, 79).[18] Other restrictions were held more consistently over time. An example of this is the generalized prohibition of same-sex marriage discussed earlier. Some of these restrictions placed on marriage thus artificially contribute to its appearance of egalitarianism: if marriage is only permitted between people who share important similarities and privileges, one can wonder whether marriage is truly a union of equals or rather a very selective and discriminatory institution. I will now expand on three major equalizing factors placed on marriage that contributed to making it an egalitarian institution in the eyes of some German jurists – which will allow me to emphasize who was included in, or excluded from, that institution.

A first example of an equalizing factor that had been placed on marriage before Kant's day was to restrict marriage to men and women of the same religious denomination. This constraint was softened over the eighteenth century: while still uncommon, marriages between partners of different religious denominations were not nearly as rare as they used to be. When more severe restrictions were put forward, privileged individuals were often able to obtain dispensations. Interconfessional marriages really only became more widespread in the general population with the introduction of civil marriage laws in late nineteenth-century Germany.[19] Another restriction remained consistently enforced throughout early

---

[18] Even though these restrictions fluctuated depending on the nature of the issues they sought to address, they consistently impacted lower-ranking soldiers and servants, to the point where many working-class individuals had no choice but to live in unmarried domestic partnerships. This made them more vulnerable in several ways, including accusations of infanticide, which, as we will see in the next section, disproportionately impacted working-class women for that reason.

[19] This remained true until the intermarriage of Jews and Christians became targeted by new restrictions in the twentieth century, such as the 1935 Law for the Protection of Blood and

modernity: that of limiting marriage to partners of similar or equal ranks. Even the 1794 Prussian legal code, for instance, required spouses to be of equal ranks, especially within nobility (Wunder 2016, 83 sq.) – although those requirements were typically loosened for a second marriage. Finally, confessional and social rank restrictions often tracked racial divides. While interracial marriages were not explicitly regulated by law until the late nineteenth century (Moses 2019, 475),[20] the restrictions on interconfessional marriages and on marriages across social classes, in addition to the additional barriers faced by working-class people, would have had important consequences for interracial couples.

Considering the discriminatory measures preventing fundamental markers of difference like faith, social class, and race from diversifying marriage, philosophers and jurists did not have too much work to do to make marriage a union of "equals." By virtue of how selective marriage was, spouses could not be too different from each other in the first place. Against this backdrop, the natural equality of the spouses, often postulated by jurists, was unlikely to be very disruptive – especially since such a shallow form of equality was, in fact, able to accommodate a significant power imbalance within the household.

Since marriage was only available to heterosexual couples, marriage theorists had to address an obvious threat to the equality of the spouses: sexual inequality. While early feminist writers had a lot to say on the matter, even jurists who had little interest or sympathy for feminist demands felt compelled to acknowledge and address gender hierarchy within marriage. By the eighteenth century, marriage was commonly construed as a contract that both partners were entering voluntarily and equally. Kant is thus not the only one construing marriage as an arrangement amongst equals.[21] Achenwall, for instance, describes marriage as a voluntary society that is simple and equal by nature. But for him and other jurists, the natural equality of the spouses is not incompatible with the authority of the husband over the wife, so long as the wife voluntarily submits to her husband: "Marriage by nature is a *voluntary society*, §. 9, that is *simple*, §. 41, and *equal*, §. 22. *On the basis of* an explicit or tacit *contract*, however, the husband can acquire the overlordship, and so the *wife* becomes the *husband's* subject" (Achenwall, 2021, Natural Law II, §42 [122]).

Honour (Moses 2019, 470). However, the Nuremberg Laws, unlike earlier restrictive laws, specifically targeted alleged racial differences rather than the differences in religious denominations.

[20] For a comprehensive overview of the new restrictions placed on interracial marriages in late nineteenth- and twentieth-century Germany, see Moses 2019 and Campt 2003.

[21] This widespread "egalitarianism" was worrisome to Justi. He criticizes the "complete equality of rights and authority for the husband and for the wife" which he argues religion seems to entail, and suggests that civil marriage might better suit the rightful "domestic power and domination" of the husband (cited in Hull 1996, 184).

Achenwall, like Kant, thus claims that spouses are naturally equal; but unlike Kant, he also explicitly justifies gender hierarchy within marriage by construing this inequality as a voluntary (yet tacit) arrangement sought by the wife. Spouses are thus naturally equal, but politically (and by choice) unequal. When the husband acquires the overlordship, the wife becomes his subject and inferior; the husband has the right to make decisions on her behalf (Achenwall, 2021, Natural Law II, §43 [122]). The husband's authority over the wife is thereby justified by the wife's consent to the arrangement. The political inequality between them is thus explicitly acknowledged and legitimized.

Since marriage was commonly understood as a contract between two equal persons of different sexes, one would assume that polygamy was simply out of the question. But Kant's mention of it in the passage from MM 6: 278 is no accident. While German jurists commonly dismissed polyandry as ridiculous, polygyny was taken more seriously, and approached through the lens of cultural relativism. Achenwall, for instance, notes, "Nature abhors *polyandry*; *polygyny* is still found in a number of nations, and there used to be quite a few peoples who indulged in communion of wives" (Achenwall, 2021, Natural Law, II, §43 [122], II, §46 [123]).

While the consensus amongst jurists was that monogamy was the better type of union (generally for pragmatic reasons: monogamy was perceived to be reducing quarrels, jealousy, and expenses within the household), polygyny was often perceived to be tracking the masculine sex drive, and given some consideration for that reason (Hull 178–179). Kant's argument that polygamy compromises the (sexual and material) equality of the partners is, in comparison, a strong and explicit criticism of polygamy.

Egalitarian arrangements within marriage were a topic that feminist authors were especially eager to write on – with much less tolerance for subordination within marriage (whether construed as natural or as the result of a voluntary arrangement). English feminist writers like Mary Astell or Mary Wollstonecraft, for instance, emphasize the importance of friendship as a pillar of marriage. While it was harder for women to publish their reflections on the matter in seventeenth- and eighteenth-century Germany than in France or England at the same period,[22] Germany also had its "querelle des femmes" (*Geschlechterstreit*); Cornelius Agrippa von Nettesheim's *Declamatio de nobilitate et praecellentia foeminei sexus* might be one of the best-known essays advocating for women's superiority in sixteenth-century Europe. Debates on marriage were an important part of the German querelle ever since the fifteenth century, and led to the production of

---

[22] Dyck expands on the hostility towards female authorship in early modern Germany (2021, 5–6).

pamphlets that were either praising women (*Frauenlob*) and supporting marriage, or scolding women (*Frauenschelte*) and denigrating marriage.[23] Women's contributions to this debate were infrequent and often took unconventional forms – philosophical essays on marriage were still uncommon.[24] Four of them, though, are worth mentioning: Marianne Ehrmann's *Philosophie eines Weibs*, Emilie von Berlepsch's *Einige zum Glueck der Ehe nothwendige Eigenschaften und Grundsätze*, and Theodor von Hippel's *Über die Ehe* and *Über die bürgerliche Verbesserung der Weiber*.[25]

German discussions of women's roles in the household and in society were especially influenced by Rousseau's account of the complementarity of the sexes. This is largely due to his broader influence on the philosophy of education in eighteenth-century Germany, which shaped the way in which gender roles were construed. Basedow, Campe, and the philanthropinist educational movement in general were considerably influenced by Rousseau's ideas on the gendered education boys and girls should receive to that end.[26] This shaped in turn the ways in which equality was considered within marriage. Sophie von la Roche, for instance, despite advocating for better educational possibilities for women, does not openly question women's traditional roles. As noted by Fronius, Emilie von Berlepsch criticizes more explicitly certain Rousseauian-inspired assumptions about feminine virtues (e.g., "the abuse of the term 'gentle'"), and commits to fighting "the prejudice according to which women neither possess their own will, nor the courage to express it" (Berlepsch 1791, 69).[27] She also warns men against despotism towards their wife:

> ... [men] will not restore by any power or genius what they destroyed by unfairness [*Unbilligkeit*] and disregard. The rule of the soul is thoroughly

---

[23] A notable contributor to the debate on marriage is Martin Luther, whose *Vom ehelichen Leben* (1522) criticizes misogynous depictions of women and marriage. For more contextual background on the German *querelle* in general, see Bock & Zimmermann 1997; Kundert 2003.

[24] For instance, Esther Gad, a Jewish feminist author, wrote a detailed response to Campe's ideas on the education of women that took an epistolary form. Around the same time, Sophie von la Roche, Friderika Baldinger, and Marianne Ehrmann also discussed women's situation and shared various insights on marriage in their novels.

[25] Interestingly enough, Hippel never got married; and there is evidence suggesting that both Ehrmann and Berlepsch were divorced. Divorce, unlike marriage, was almost never discussed in written works at the time – despite the fact that it became fairly common throughout the eighteenth century in Germany and that many famous women writers (e.g. Dorothea Schlegel, Sophie Mereau, Caroline Schelling) got divorced. As to how this relates to feminist works on marriage, one could wonder if, maybe, writers like Ehrmann, Berlepsch, and Hippel simply had high standards for a successful marriage.

[26] See on this Louden's excellent essay on Amalia Holst's reception of Basedow and Campe's ideas (2021).

[27] My discovery of Berlepsch's ideas is indebted to Helen Fronius' excellent analysis in *The Diligent Dilettante: Women Writers in Germany 1770–1820*, 2003, 249–253. While Fronius

republican in nature, and is bound to degenerate into wild anarchy as soon as it acquires a despotic appearance and wants to base itself merely on the right of the strongest. (Berlepsch 1791, 76)

This warning does not entail that the household is an entirely egalitarian space with respect to power distribution, but rather that power dynamics should remain fair and balanced. Berlepsch does not completely renounce gender roles and responsibilities, and even preserves a certain form of authority for the husband over the wife: he is still entitled to "direct her soul," so long as he is wise enough to know how to nurture her abilities, inclinations, and powers (Berlepsch 1791, 76). But she also encourages women to acquire, beyond questionable feminine virtues, a form of intellectual independence (*Selbstständigkeit*) to better protect themselves against men. This independence is reminiscent of the Enlightenment ideal of thinking for oneself: Berlepsch is hoping for women to learn to stand up for themselves and to trust their own judgment over prejudice or the judgment of others (Berlepsch 1791, 89–90). So while Berlepsch avoids talking about equality in the household, she unquestionably advocates for women to gain more control over their own lives, rather than being entirely subordinated to their husband.[28]

It would be odd to discuss legal and feminist perspectives on gender equality and marriage without engaging with Theodor von Hippel's contribution. While Hippel also embraces a Rousseauian-inspired ideal of complementarity between the sexes, his treatise *Über die bürgerliche Verbesserung der Weiber* demonstrates an especially clear commitment to a form of complementary-based radical egalitarianism in marriage. Hippel's proposed reform of marriage is grounded in a broader reflection on sexual inequality. While the young Hippel already questioned the prejudice of the inferiority of women in a 1768 speech delivered to his Freemason lodge, his treatise *Über die Ehe*, first published in 1774, still presented relatively conservative views on gender roles and power dynamics in marriage. Later reeditions reflect the evolution of his views, which came to fruition with the publication of *Über die bürgerliche Verbesserung der Weiber* in 1792, in which he takes a clear stance against any speculations on the inferiority of women, and emphasizes the

---

reads Berlepsch through a more egalitarian lens than I do, she rightly emphasizes the novelty and radicality of Berlepsch's thought.

[28] Dawson suggests that Berlepsch may be hoping, through this plea for independence, to gradually change women's role in society (Dawson 1986, 166). Berlepsch's example is also a good reminder that feminist contributions have taken multiple forms throughout history: while her discussion of the possibility of a rightful authority of the husband over the wife would likely not hold well from a contemporary feminist perspective, for instance, it still provides a strong criticism of gendered power dynamics.

radical implications of the natural equality of men and women.[29] Hippel extensively discusses this natural equality – not limiting it, like other jurists, to a nominal form of equality as human beings, but rather explicitly extending it to the equal possession of reason in men and women.[30] Hippel also expands on the consequences of this idea. Since women and men are equal in reason, women should be entitled to a proper education and civil rights, including the possibility of joining the workforce[31], and they should also be regarded as the equal of men in marriage. Marriage, rather than being considered in isolation, is thus one of many institutions standing in need of reform. Hippel tasks himself with rethinking these institutions on the grounds of the fundamental equality of men and women. In the case of marriage, this equality should be reflected in the distribution of power and authority in the household:

> Have we forgotten already that marriage is an institution of equals [*eine gleiche Gesellschaft*], that authority in marriage must remain the reciprocal authority of the spouses on one another, and that the man can only claim his wife as his own by means of an *express* agreement? (Hippel 2009, 205; modified translation)

Hippel's robust conception of gender equality entails that authority, in marriage, is not the sole prerogative of the husband, but rather should be shared between the spouses in a mutual way. While not rejecting the idea altogether, Hippel is also nuancing the possibility that a woman may consent to her husband having complete authority over her: such an arrangement can only take place if she gives an *express*, or explicit, agreement to it. This emphasis is likely a response to the stance of jurists like Achenwall who, as we have seen, justify the subordination of the wife to the husband by resorting to the idea of a tacit

---

[29] In addition to his background and experience as a jurist, several political factors may have contributed to this evolution of Hippel's thought. For instance, Pascoe extensively discusses the influence of the 1791 Prussian Legal Code and its impact on the reeditions of Hippel's *Über die Ehe* (Pascoe 2018, 237n18). The reforms proposed by the Code were also inspired, to some extent, by the French Revolution – which also considerably affected Hippel's views. In his 1792 treatise, Hippel speaks highly of the French Revolution for its diffusion of Enlightenment ideals, but also criticizes it harshly for leaving women outside of the scope of these ideals: "How could a people which exists *by* and *for* the fair sex […] neglect, in their proclamation of general equality which has been acclaimed throughout the earth, a sex possessing a queen with doubtless few equals in the world?" (Hippel 2009, 141, 219) For Hippel, there is now no doubt that citizens' rights should be extended to men and women alike.

[30] Hippel's demonstration of the natural equality of men and women is grounded in his interpretation of the Fall, by which he establishes that Eve, rather than being at fault, is in fact responsible for the breakthrough of reason. I analyze Hippel's argument and its implications in more detail in Sabourin 2021b, 167–172.

[31] Hippel is here thinking of women as doctors, judges, or instructors – but perhaps should have acknowledged that many women (working-class women) were already part of the workforce in different roles.

consent provided by the wife (cf. Achenwall, 2021, Natural Law II, §42 [122]). Hippel calls such tacit consent a "silent sin." In the end, dividing the authority between the two spouses still seems to be the better solution: "Men and women both gain equally through a divided rule in the home" (Hippel 2009, 383). While Kant postulates the equality of men and women *as spouses*, specifically in the context of his discussion of marriage, Hippel's late reflections on marriage are thus the consequence of a deeper commitment to gender equality. In other words: for Kant, marriage requires a certain form of equality, whereas for Hippel, a robust conception of equality must precede (and shape) marriage.[32]

While the egalitarian nature of Kant's account of marriage can be partly explained by broader conversations amongst jurists on marriage and natural equality, it is unlikely that he would have had no awareness of the more feminist discussions taking place around the equality of spouses. We can assume that he had no interest in partaking in them: while he appreciated the company of women in social contexts, he notoriously refused to discuss social or political matters with them (Stuckenberg 1882, 183 sq.).[33] He also made plenty of derogatory remarks on women. Kant was also notoriously critical of *Popularphilosophie*, a genre reminiscent of today's public philosophy, which was typically better suited to social and political demands like the ones voiced by Hippel, Berlepsch, or Ehrmann. But given his long-time friendship with Theodor von Hippel, he would at the very least have heard of some of the questions preoccupying the later. While his own stance on the equality of the spouses is clearly not motivated by feminist considerations, it has likely been shaped not only by juridical, but also by feminist conversations.

3 On Those Who Did Not Marry: Kant and the Infanticide Debate

Having discussed the ways in which accounts of marriage in eighteenth-century Germany engaged with the idea of spousal equality, and having analyzed the divide between feminists and jurists regarding the nature and implications of this equality, it now seems important to take a step back and reflect on the serious consequences of gender inequality beyond the boundaries of marriage. This will allow for a reflection on the implications of being excluded from this institution, and highlight the necessity of adding broader social reforms to

---

[32] The contrast between Hippel's late account of marriage and Kant's is extensively discussed by Hull (1996, 301–332) and by Pascoe (2018). Pascoe helpfully frames Hippel's account of marriage as a civic partnership, entirely political in nature, whereas Kant's account of marriage is a juridical institution that must regulate our natural needs – and has in that sense a pre-political component (Pascoe 2017, 227).

[33] There are a few exceptions to this rule in Kant's correspondence – for instance, his response to Maria von Herbert (11:331 sq.) – but not many.

reforms of marriage like the one proposed by Kant. I will focus specifically on the prosecution of unwed mothers for infanticide, a concrete issue that captures many of these concerns and that Kant himself found significant enough to address.

Beyond Kant, eighteenth-century Germany was marked by a widespread concern for infanticide, which was assumed to be the byproduct of fornication and thus associated with out-of-wedlock pregnancies. Infanticide was, for that reason, prosecuted very differently amongst different groups of people. Men, married or unmarried, were seldom accused of infanticide.[34] Married women were also rarely found guilty of infanticide (as they were presumed to have no motive) – and those who were, were granted lighter sentences (Uleman 2000, 179). Unmarried women, on the other hand, were generally sentenced to death. Infanticide is, as such, an issue of special interest to women, and more specifically to the more vulnerable working-class women, who were often unable or even forbidden to enter marriage. This preoccupation was reflected in the Enlighteners' growing concern for infanticide – Kant's discussion of infanticide, like many others, specifically focuses on unwed mothers. From a contemporary feminist perspective, infanticide is thus a relevant topic to consider when thinking about marriage and its exclusions in early modern Germany. In what follows, I will first show that the institution of marriage was not equally accessible to all, and explain why infanticides were so closely associated with unmarried women. I will then turn to Kant's remarks in the *Doctrine of Right*. I argue that while Kant does not, in the end, show mercy to the women accused of infanticide, his ambivalent stance reveals that he had at least some awareness of how difficult their situation was, due to the presumed loss of their honour combined with their unmarried status. I will finally turn to feminist reflections on infanticide by Marianne Ehrmann and Theodor von Hippel, which both emphasize the inequalities that unmarried women were bound to face in the patriarchal society they knew and provide a helpful contrast with Kant's views.

From the medieval dowry system in Europe to the prohibition of interracial marriages or of same-sex marriages up to recent days in North America, the institution of marriage has always relied on the exclusion of certain groups of people. Kant's own case is worth reflecting on. As is widely known, Kant never married, and that decision may have partly been financial, as he would have had a hard time providing for a wife and children for most of his active life. Following his father's death in 1746,

---

[34] Lewis mentions the cases of Samuel Keck and Jeremias Bertz as rare examples of men who were convicted for infanticide and executed on those grounds. She emphasizes that unlike most "child-murderesses," Keck and Bertz were depicted in an almost heroic manner (Lewis 2016, 168 sq.).

22-year-old Kant had to support his siblings. He first worked as a private tutor until he obtained his Magister degree in 1755, at which point he was authorized to teach university courses – but without a salary (Kuehn 2001, 94–105; see also Correspondence p. 6). While he might have once had some interest in getting married, there are indications that he ended up feeling like he had missed that boat.[35]

Kant's case, while far from being unique, was also not the direst: throughout the early modern period, economic circumstances frequently dictated who got to get married, and to whom. In addition to regulations affecting the whole population (such as the parental consent required by some local legislations in Germany), certain towns and states imposed a minimal income or property ownership as a precondition to entering marriage. Servants and other working-class individuals were especially affected by these restrictions. In Bavaria, for instance, the legal age of marriage for servants was raised in order to make up for labour shortages (Wunder 2016, 79). When faced with the impossibility to get married, many servants and workers still chose to live in cohabitation with a significant other. This further exposed unmarried working-class women to accusations of infanticide. Unmarried women were required by law to declare their pregnancy (others were encouraged to report them if they didn't), and any out-of-wedlock pregnancy that was not carried to term could in theory be scrutinized as a possible case of abortion or infanticide. While abortion was also criminalized, it was typically not prosecuted to the same degree as infanticide. Jurists were aware that it was much more difficult to prove in a court of law – the main difference between (self-inflicted) abortion and miscarriage being a matter of intention. The stakes were also different, as the Church did not systematically regard abortion as murder. Fetal life was only considered human life after the process of ensoulment – which, depending on the sex of the fetus, would occur between the 40th day and the 90th day of pregnancy (Eser 1986, 370). Abortion and infanticide were thus treated separately in Prussian legislations.[36] This does not entail, of course, that the difference between infanticide and miscarriage was any easier to establish: up to the late eighteenth

---

[35] "He himself is said to have quipped that when he could have benefited from being married, he could not afford it, and when he could afford it, he could no longer have benefited from it" (Kuehn 2001, 117).

[36] On the history of the prosecution of abortion in Germany, see Lewis 2016, 29 sq., and Eser 1986, 369. Lewis also helpfully notes that abortion, like pregnancy, was seen as a private matter – the aggressive prosecution of abortion being perceived, in that context, as an intrusion into family life. As a consequence, married women were much less likely to be prosecuted for abortion or infanticide than unmarried women, in order to avoid intruding into the husband's privacy. A common thread between this superficial (and relative) permissibility of abortion and today's anti-abortion movements is that either way, women are dispossessed from control over their own bodies and reproductive rights – whether it is for the benefit of a husband, lineage, or society.

century, German physicians were still using the *Lungenprobe*, a medical test used to determine whether a baby was born alive or dead, in cases of suspected infanticides. While this test was widely known to be unreliable, it frequently served as evidence leading to the conviction of women for infanticide – and also at times to exonerate others.

In light of these complex circumstances and of the inaccuracy of most investigation methods, it seems clear that most women who were prosecuted for infanticide were far from the stereotype of the cold-blooded or insane child murderess. While the latter type was much more mediatized, infanticide accusations also led to the execution of very different types of women. There were, for instance, women who had simply suffered a miscarriage. There were also, as noted by Adrienne Rich, women who were placed in terrible, no-win situations, and who resorted to infanticide (voluntarily or not) because they had no other choice:

> Throughout history numberless women have killed children they knew they could not rear, whether economically or emotionally, children forced upon them by rape, ignorance, poverty, marriage, or by the absence of, or sanctions against, birth control and abortion. (Rich 1995, 258)

Amongst these we can count women who were raped and unsuccessfully went through painful rounds of self-inflicted abortions, women who were forced to give their own food to their older children so that they could survive, being as a result unable to breastfeed their newborn baby, and women who knew all too well about foundling homes' low survival rate and atrocious living conditions (Lewis 2016, 44).[37] These women, Rich argues, deserve our compassion too, and their lives and crimes may teach us something about the deep flaws of the patriarchal institution of motherhood. Accusations of infanticide are a painful reminder that being excluded from the institution of marriage could be very costly for those who were already vulnerable and did not benefit from the same protection others received. The wide range of circumstances leading to infanticide (or presumed infanticide) emphasized by Rich also reflects the specific hardships that women are bound to face in a society that does not adequately support them in their care work or provide access to reproductive health resources. While Kant was not particularly interested in this last range of issues, we will see that they informed a wide range of perspectives on infanticide.

Germany's concern for infanticide in Kant's day is interesting given that the rate of reported infanticides was in fact not especially high (Hull 1996, 112). But the highly publicized executions of *Kindsmörderin*, women found guilty of

---

[37] Unmarried women, unlike married couples, were not allowed to place their baby in a regular orphanage, where living conditions and chances of survival were better.

having killed their child, made an impression on public opinion and prompted scholars, writers, and politicians to weigh in. Most of them were attempting to promote clemency towards the defendants and an increased tolerance towards fornication. For instance, the journal *Rheinische Beiträge zur Gelehrsamkeit* issued the following prize essay question in 1780, which prompted hundreds of contributions: "What are the best and most practical means to prevent infanticide without encouraging fornication?"[38] This widespread concern also led to several law reforms decriminalizing fornication as a harm-reduction measure: Prussia, for instance, decriminalized it in 1765 for pregnant women. Frederick the Great and many Enlightenment thinkers were especially preoccupied by the social causes presumably leading to infanticide. Their reasoning was that a pregnancy was placing unmarried working-class women in an especially dire position: they would have to face public shaming and fines for the illegitimate pregnancy, in addition to the unlikelihood of being able to provide for themselves and for their child in the absence of support from the father or his family. Other factors might have contributed to this wave of compassion for the pressure placed on poor, unmarried women: as emphasized in my earlier discussion of marriage, Enlighteners were also interested in defining or redefining the role of the state in regulating sexuality.[39] The presumed connection between illegitimate pregnancies and infanticides was, however, never really questioned until the nineteenth century. To the Enlighteners, showing leniency towards the women accused of infanticide generally implied being more permissive of fornication, and conversely.

One would think that the increased concern for the social causes leading to infanticide would result in the removal of death penalty for convicted women. But most Enlighteners considered that if some work had been done upstream to address the social causes leading one to commit infanticide, a severe punishment was all the more justified for the crime. While works on infanticide often shared compassion for the unfortunate mother, this compassion thus rarely resulted in a plea for her life.[40] Kant's reflections on infanticide reveal a similar struggle.

While Kant was in general not especially sensitive to the obstacles faced by unwed pregnant women, he did weigh in on the infanticide debate, and in

---

[38] *Rheinische Beiträge zur Gelehrsamkeit* 1780, vol 2 (July). See also Hull 1996, 111.
[39] Michalik notes that Frederick the Great likely also had pragmatic considerations in mind, as Prussia was facing a wave of depopulation during his reign: Being less repressive of illegitimate pregnancies could contribute to increasing the birth rate (Michalik 2006, 54). This supports the argument made by Rich and other feminist philosophers: Birth control, abortion, and infanticide-related legislations are impacted by other political and demographic considerations, such as the desire to recruit cheap labour, the concern for a low birth rate, etc. (Rich 1995, 271).
[40] Michalik's research emphasizes that convictions became more severe under Frederick the Great: Up to 1765, convicted women were sentenced to jail rather than to the death penalty if the child's death was presumably due to neglect (Michalik 2006, 56).

a way that makes clear he construed infanticide as an issue specifically relevant to unmarried women. Kant's discussion of infanticide has generated many comprehensive contributions – by Baier (1993), Uleman (2000), Sussman (2008), Varden (2020), Pascoe (2011), and Timmermann (2022). While there is no consensus regarding how best to interpret Kant's final thoughts on the matter, commentators are generally unimpressed with Kant's lack of sensitivity in handling the issue.[41] Here I want to show that Kant's reflections on infanticide are relevant to his account of marriage: Kant, like his peers, situates his discussion of infanticide outside the boundaries of marriage. This special focus is intentional, as he takes infanticide to be an issue raising unique moral complications for unmarried women – which does not, however, absolve them from the punishment any other person convicted with murder would receive.

Kant's discussion of infanticide is introduced as a follow-up to his discussion of capital punishment. Kant argues in the *Doctrine of Right* that punishments granted in a court of law must follow the law of retribution: murderers must receive a death sentence. He also anticipates a few objections to that rule. First, there are cases in which the law of retribution cannot be straightforwardly applied: for instance, it would not make sense to impose a fine to a thief to punish them for stealing someone else's property if they are too poor to pay the fine. They may be sentenced to prison labour instead – which would preserve the spirit of the *ius talionis*, if not the letter. Kant's endorsement of the death penalty on the grounds of retributive justice, while regrettable, was not surprising at the time: Cesare Beccaria was the main dissenting voice arguing for the abolition of capital punishment. Kant briefly addresses Beccaria's stance: while a person sentenced to death may well prefer not to be executed, this does not contradict the idea that the general will still supports the resort to death penalty for someone who has been convicted of murder (MM 6: 335).

Kant then takes his argument one step further by introducing two cases that, he suggests, *may* warrant making an exception to the law of retribution: the duellist who kills a fellow soldier, and the mother who kills her own child. Kant's question is not whether infanticide is a crime that merits punishment (he thinks it is), but rather whether death is an appropriate punishment in that case, and whether legislation is legitimate in imposing that punishment or not. While

---

[41] One notable exception to this is Varden who, while agreeing that Kant holds homicidal mothers accountable for their crime and that the law of retribution calls, in theory, for death penalty, argues that Kant also holds that they cannot be rightly punished in situations deemed unrightful – which is the case as long as the mother and the child are doomed to a life in poverty and shame due to current social norms (Varden 2020, 233–234).

his reasons for discussing the two examples together are not entirely clear, Kant relates both crimes to similar honour-related motivations:[42]

> The feeling of honor leads to both, in one case the *honor of one's sex*, in the other *military honor*, and indeed true honor, which is incumbent as duty on each of these two classes of people. The one crime is a mother's *murder of her child* (*infanticidium maternale*); the other is *murdering a fellow soldier* (*commilitonicidium*) in a duel.

In framing infanticide as an honour crime,[43] Kant emphasizes the gender- and class-related dimensions of the issue: his account of infanticide only applies to unmarried women – who, he assumes, resort to infanticide in order to get rid of the evidence of their supposedly dishonourable sexual behaviour. Throughout this passage, Kant is chiefly interested in the tension between the objective justice of the state and the people's subjective perception of what is just – a tension that he admittedly handles in an ambivalent way, as pointed out by Pascoe (2011). Two different explanations are proposed in the *Doctrine of Right*. The first one, criticized for its cruelty despite its plea to spare the mother's life, is in fact not Kant's own proposed resolution but rather one he disagrees with. Timmermann has convincingly demonstrated that point (2022, 13–14), but I hope to shed some more light on Kant's interlocutor here. The second proposed course of action may remain unsatisfying in other ways, as it reiterates that the mother must be sentenced to death – but it at least captures Kant's own views.

Kant first introduces a possible way of judging infanticides that he in fact does not endorse. However, due to the popularity of this reasoning, he likely felt compelled to address it. It consists in arguing that the illegitimate child does not count as a person in the eyes of the state – which Pascoe captures as the lack of *juridical* personality, that is being recognized by the state as a person entitled to certain rights and a legal protection, whether one is an active citizen or a passive one (2011, 7) – and, therefore, that the mother should not be convicted for murder:

> So it seems that in these two cases people find themselves in the state of nature, and that these acts of killing (*homicidium*), which would then not even have to

---

[42] Timmermann notes that Kant's juxtaposition of the two cases may have been suggested by Frederick the Great's combined discussion of the two cases in a 1749 treatise (2022, 5–6).

[43] Timmermann supplements this passage by turning to earlier fragments in which Kant discusses the notion of a "point of honour," which, in the case of unmarried women, revolves around chastity. This point of honour is deemed more important to one's eyes than one's own life, thus affecting the perspective one may have of a death sentence. (Timmermann 2022, 7) This last point (one's honour being valued more than one's own life) is also reiterated in the *Doctrine of Right*, MM 6: 334.

be called murder (*homicidium dolosum*), are certainly punishable but cannot be punished with death by the supreme power. A child that comes into the world apart from marriage is born outside the law (for the law is marriage) and therefore outside the protection of the law. It has, as it were, stolen into the commonwealth (like contraband merchandise), so that the commonwealth can ignore its existence (since it rightly should not have come to exist in this way), and can therefore also ignore its annihilation; and no decree can remove the mother's shame when it becomes known that she gave birth without being married. (MM 6: 336)

This reasoning has been portrayed as cruel (Baier 1993, 446): suggesting that the mother should not be convicted for murder – not out of mercy, or compassion for the adverse circumstances she has been facing, or lack of evidence, but rather because the human being she was accused of killing does not count as a legal person and is thus not entitled to the protection of the state, is insensitive. But the argument is not Kant's own, and it's not clear that he endorses it (since he argues, in the end, for the opposite conclusion: infanticide is a crime that should be punished with death penalty).[44] Amongst other stylistic and philosophical indications, Timmermann's detailed discussion of the passage notes that Kant introduces this reasoning in a hypothetical way ("*So it seems that* in these two cases people find themselves in the state of nature ... ") and that he also separates it from the rest of his argument using two long dashes (Timmermann 2022, 14).[45] Timmermann suggests this hypothetical argument may be directed at Beccaria, thus extending the conversation started in MM 6: 334. While I agree that Kant is playing devil's advocate rather than presenting an argument he actually endorses, I believe Kant is addressing a specific argument put forward, not by Beccaria, but rather during the publicized trial of Margaretha von Kawatschinska, a Polish woman accused of double infanticide and sentenced to death, who then appealed of her sentence in 1791. While the prosecution was recommending death penalty on the grounds of Kawatschinska having deprived the state of Prussia (which had then a relatively small population) of two potential citizens, her defense argued that the children should not count as citizens since they were born out of wedlock.[46] Kant would have been

---

[44] I am not arguing here that Kant does not find parts of this argument compelling – but rather, that he disagrees with its conclusion. Pascoe (2011) rightly notes, for instance, that his description of the illegitimate child's lack of innate rights maps onto a notion of juridical personhood that is consistent with Kant's conception of right. The way in which Kant lays out this argument is also consistent, as she points out, with the idea that legal rights and protections require recognition by the state (2011, 4). Pascoe also helpfully uses Kant's conception of legal rights in relation to the passage in MM 6: 336 sq. to argue for a right to voluntary motherhood in a subsequent article (2019).

[45] Timmermann also refers to Brandt 1999, 279, who makes a similar hypothesis.

[46] See Hippel 2009, 541 n3.

familiar with the case, as his friend Theodor von Hippel served as judge during one of Kawatschinska's trials.[47] Hippel, who ended up supporting the death sentence, remained deeply troubled by the case and published an essay discussing his thoughts on it, which I turn to at the end of this section. But it is worth citing here some of his thoughts on the main argument used by the defense: "Should the notion that a child was conceived outside of marriage and, therefore, outside the bounds of civil society render this case less severe in the eyes of the state?" (Hippel 2009, 403) For Hippel, the argument that the state does not owe legal protection to illegitimate children does not constitute sufficient grounds to spare Kawatschinska the death sentence she would otherwise receive – despite second thoughts he may have had about applying capital punishment in this case. Kant likely agrees with Hippel's analysis here, even though we may wish he had said more about it.

Kant then introduces his own reasoning. Penal justice finds itself in a quandary here, he says, because:

> either it must declare by law that the concept of honor (which is here no illusion) counts for nothing and so punish with death, or else it must remove from the crime the capital punishment appropriate to it, and so be either cruel or indulgent (MM 6: 336).

On the one hand, Kant acknowledges that the existence of the illegitimate child constitutes evidence of the loss of the mother's honour (if it becomes known that she gave birth to a child out of wedlock) – and that this loss of honour is itself punished by the law, making the law cruel. On the other hand, if criminal justice does not punish the infanticide as murder, it fails to do its job – applying the law of retribution. This shows that Kant acknowledges the conflict between social and legal norms experienced by unwed mothers – thus adopting, in that sense, a surprisingly compassionate standpoint, as noted by Uleman (2000, 174, 192).[48] Kant rarely acknowledges or addresses discrepancies between theory and practice – his doing so regarding the fate of unwed mothers accused of infanticide is thus especially noteworthy. But the way in which he resolves the dilemma seems less compassionate, for he upholds capital punishment in the end:

---

[47] It is also worth noting that Johann Daniel Metzger (who Kant knew well but was not always on good terms with) served as expert medical advisor on the case of von Kawatschinska (Gerlings 2017, 159 sq.).

[48] This reading is shared to some degree by Pascoe (2019, 5), who puts forward a critical appropriation of Kant's views in order to define the legal status of the fetus and the rights of the mother. The intuition that Kant's stance is more compassionate than he is often perceived to be has also greatly inspired Varden's work (especially her 2020 monograph).

> The knot can be undone in the following way: The categorical imperative of penal justice remains (unlawful killing of another must be punished by death); but the legislation itself (and consequently also the civil constitution), as long as it remains barbarous and undeveloped, is responsible for the discrepancy between the incentives [*Triebfedern*] of honor in the people (subjectively) and the measures that are (objectively) suitable for its purpose. (MM 6: 336–337)

I, like Timmermann, have little doubt that in this passage Kant confirms that the *ius talionis* must apply in the case of trials for infanticide: "unlawful killing of another must be punished by death." The caveat he adds pertains to the ways in which current imperfect legislations often fail to reconcile the subjective motives of honour in the people with the measures that may objectively be put forward to that end (legal punishments and rewards). But this passage deserves further clarification.

At first glance, the case of the mother accused of infanticide seems to capture a deeper conflict of duties between the duty of preserving one's honour and the duty of not killing another being. Kant himself concedes that being an honourable person, which consists in not making oneself a mere means for others, may be regarded as a duty of right (MM 6: 236). Similar to other examples of conflicts of duties, the conflict is only apparent: the unmarried woman is not forced to choose between saving her honour and sparing her child's life. Her honour, by Kant's unforgiving criterion, has already been compromised by having unmarried sex. Killing the illegitimate child is thus merely a way of concealing this supposed loss of honour – and by no means a way of gaining her honour back.[49] Holding subjective appearances of honour to be more valuable than one's child's life (or one's own life, since death sentence is to apply) is thus a mistake. But this misunderstanding is not the mother's sole responsibility. It is the result of politics encouraging one to conceal their illegitimate pregnancy – presumably to save their honour, as well as to avoid fines and other secular penalties punishing fornication,[50] in addition to the ongoing social stigma and the financial hardship that a single mother would face for raising a child out of wedlock. These strong subjective incitements to conceal one's loss of honour thus make the punishment imposed for infanticide come across as unjust. In a better state (and perhaps Kant thought that Frederick's reforms would cause

---

[49] In that sense, I disagree with Sussman's reading of Kant's conception of honour: it seems dangerous to infer that we have something like a right to defend our honour and our reputation (Sussman 2008, 302). While this reasoning might make more sense of the duelist's situation, the unwed mother is not defending her honour by killing her child: She is merely hiding evidence of her dishonour.

[50] This specific measure was abolished by Frederick II in 1765, as Kant would have known. Regarding the measures put in place to dissuade fornication, see Wunder's detailed analysis of marriage in the Holy Roman Empire (Wunder 2016, 79) and Hull 1996, 115.

improvement in this respect), the gap would gradually close: people would have a better sense of where true honour lies rather than being pressured into hiding a loss of honour, and would thus not perceive the punishment of infanticide to be at odds with social expectations.

This confirms that, for Kant, infanticide is an issue that holds particular implications for unmarried women. I doubt that Kant would have been fine with the lighter sentences given to married women or men accused of infanticide: for him, infanticide remains murder, and as such, must be punished proportionally. But unmarried pregnant women find themselves in a unique double bind – because they face the risk of being exposed for having lost their honour, which came with harsh consequences in eighteenth-century Prussia. While we may regret that Kant did not extend his compassion to waiving death penalty in this case, his discussion of the matter highlights that being excluded from the institution of marriage in a patriarchal society carries significant risks and penalties.

I will finally turn to two feminist reflections on infanticide: Hippel's essay on the trial and execution of Margaretha von Kawatschinska, and Ehrmann's infanticide fiction "Die unglückliche Hanne." I will show that like Kant, Ehrmann and Hippel identify and attempt to address the unique hardship faced by unmarried working-class women in infanticide trials, and that their emotional responses to the problem are very different. While Hippel and Ehrmann do not dispute that capital punishment is right in the circumstances, they capture much more eloquently their discomfort at this idea.

I have mentioned earlier that the main argument used by the defense of Margaretha von Kawatschinska likely influenced Kant's discussion of the sentence granted for infanticide. Her trial and execution made quite an impression on the public, and led Hippel to publish a 134-page long essay on her story in 1792: "Report Concerning the Von K . . . Case; a Contribution to the Question of Crime and Punishment." Hippel's discussion of the case is informed by his background as a judge, while also being intended for a broader audience. While the essay shares important similarities with Kant's views, it is, in the end, a much more emotional piece that manages to capture how conflicted his author was regarding death penalty.

While Hippel does not advocate for the complete abolition of capital punishment, he shares Kant's retributive conception of justice, and argues, like him, that death penalty should be reserved only for the worst sorts of crimes.[51] Hippel also wonders, like Kant, whether some proposed alternatives to capital punishment might in fact be less humane – in this case, the practice of exiling prisoners to Siberia or to Australia. And not unlike Kant, Hippel defers to

---

[51] Hippel also takes Beccaria to be promoting a retributive conception of justice and punishment allowing for the use of death penalty to punish the worst crimes, which seems to be a stretch of Beccaria's views (Hippel 2009, 403).

existing Prussian laws regarding the appropriate punishment granted for infanticides (in order to dismiss arguments like the one put forward by Kawatschinska's defense).

Despite these similarities, Hippel reveals to be far more conflicted regarding the use of death penalty in cases like Kawatschinska's. Unlike Kant's, Hippel's conception of retributive justice does not solely focus on assessing the gravity of the offense: it should also weigh in the various hardships and life circumstances that may have driven the offender to perpetrate a crime: "We should judge the severity of the crime according to the degree of freedom of choice possessed by the person who committed the crime, as well as by the circumstances surrounding his or her probable motives" (Hippel 2009, 403).

In the case of the wave of infanticides affecting mostly working-class, single women, Hippel seems open to considering socio-economic factors as mitigating circumstances, thus bringing Kant's concern about the discrepancy between subjective incentives of honour and legal sentences to more concrete grounds.[52] Hippel notes that poverty and fear of disgrace are important motives for infanticides in women – and that they could easily be abolished by better institutions, which is consistent with the broader reforms he was eager to put forward. This reflection does not lead Hippel to reconsider altogether the outcome of Kawatschinska's case (likely because she was accused not only of one, but of two separate infanticides) – but it certainly shows that he is conflicted about it. He expresses sympathy for her, and acknowledges that she sought desperate measures due to the desperate situation she was placed in – thus making it difficult to ascribe an adequate and just punishment. Hippel also seems eager to question the way in which unmarried women were more harshly punished than married women – also consistently with Kant's view. Due to a bizarre Prussian law, any prisoner sentenced to death was able to appeal of their sentence if they received a marriage proposal during their trial – which happened to Kawatschinska. Hippel cynically explains this law by pointing to the interest of the state in promoting marriage, while making clear that he considers it a questionable motive to soften someone's sentence (Hippel 2009, 404).

The last contribution on infanticide that I will contrast with Kant's was written by Marianne Ehrmann, one of the very first women journalists in Germany. Ehrmann embraced early feminist beliefs even more openly than Hippel: she wrote on women's education and ran the first women's magazine in

---

[52] It might be worth noting that Hippel was also in favour of assessing whether the convicted woman was modest enough, notably by looking at her character and also at her mother's situation (!) – but he fortunately nuanced this by emphasizing that these considerations should not settle the case on their own (Hippel 2009, 404).

Germany. Ehrmann also published an epistolary novel, *Amalie, Eine wahre Geschichte in Briefen*, that is largely autobiographical and in which she proposes a feminist reflection on divorce. Ehrmann's contribution to the infanticide debate takes the form of an infanticide fiction, a genre that became increasingly popular in the *Sturm und Drang* movement: Goethe and Schiller, for instance, published famous infanticide fictions (*Urfaust* and *Die Kindsmörderin*).

While most infanticide fictions were intended to serve as warnings against the dangers of seduction and fornication,[53] Marianne Ehrmann published one that served different purposes. Her short story, "Die unglückliche Hanne" (1790), focuses on the struggle of a maid, Hanne, who is seduced by a man, Karl Schwammer, gets pregnant out of wedlock, and as a result, is jailed with her child. Hanne ultimately decides to kill her daughter to spare her the suffering she expects her to encounter in the world as a woman, and then gets executed. While it was not unusual for infanticide fictions to revolve around the torments of the protagonist, Ehrmann's infanticide fiction is unusual in two major ways: first, in how Ehrmann brings to light and emphasizes the economic hardship faced by the protagonist, and second, with respect to the anger Hanne openly expresses at her situation and at her seducer.[54] "Die unglückliche Hanne" thus grounds its analysis of infanticide in significant reflections on the specific obstacles faced by women in society. For instance, Hanne frequently refers to Karl as a monster (*Ungeheuer*) and shares about her anger in the following passage:

> You do not know us women well enough; unbridled rage when confronted with insults in love is just as part of us as gentle angelic kindness in trust, which once chained me to you! – Yes, there was a time when you told me about love, but now has come the time when I tell you about curses! (Ehrmann 1790, 128)

Ehrmann does not merely depict the tragic downfall of a seduced heroine in her infanticide fiction: she gives her a voice and, through her, expresses anger at the hardships faced by women in society and, indirectly, at the romanticized way in which infanticides were usually portrayed.

Ehrmann's infanticide fiction thus captures some of the challenges faced by unmarried women: the dangers of unlawful unions gone wrong, but also the lack

---

[53] Madland (1989) notes that infanticide fictions were unlikely to be successful in that respect, since most of the women convicted for infanticide were working-class women and illiterate, while the women reading infanticide fictions were typically issued from middle- or upper-class backgrounds. She further argues that infanticide fictions were in fact participating in the subordination, intimidation, and domestication of women by enforcing a specific conception of femininity.

[54] Madland (1992) provides an especially extensive analysis of Ehrmann's *Die unglückliche Hanne*, emphasizing these distinctive features.

of protection and support that they and their illegitimate child can expect. Like Kant and Hippel, Ehrmann's account shows that unmarried women are placed in an especially difficult situation regarding accusations of infanticide. And also like Kant and Hippel, Ehrmann does not question the death sentence granted to her protagonist – but she makes sure to emphasize the cruelty of the situation that Hanne was put through. Although fictional, her narrative provides a remarkably profound insight into the agency of the condemned woman, which is a perspective that neither Kant nor Hippel were especially eager to explore.

Through this analysis of Kant's account of infanticide against the backdrop of the circumstances in which German Enlighteners became interested in the matter, I hope to have shown that his account is perhaps not as cruel as it is sometimes taken to be: Kant does not, in the end, argue that the life of illegitimate children is worth less than that of any other child, and Kant also acknowledges that there is an overwhelming tension between social expectations for unmarried women and the prosecution of infanticide from a legal standpoint. In doing so, Kant's account of infanticide reveals that he is aware of the special protection marriage grants to those who can enter it: the conundrum in which unmarried women are placed if they get pregnant does not have an equivalent for married women or for men, who are not at risk of being exposed for having lost their honour. However, in light of Hippel and Ehrmann's insights on the socio-economic circumstances surrounding the recourse to infanticide, I have also shown that Kant's account carries some important limitations. While Hippel, like Kant, promotes a retributive conception of justice, he makes much more room for the accused' personal circumstances to be factored into the assessment of the gravity of the crime – thus opening the door to reconsidering capital punishment in at least some cases of infanticides, even if not in Kawatschinska's case. And while Ehrmann does not dispute that the maid Hanne should be sentenced to death, she offers more sympathetic insights on what might lead a woman to commit infanticide, beyond the abstract idea of a loss of honour.[55]

4 Kant and the Community of Marriage

The previous sections have shed light on key debates surrounding the institution of marriage that have significantly influenced Kant's perspective. Understanding

---

[55] It is worth noting that neither Kant, nor Hippel, nor Ehrmann seem especially interested in reflecting on the possibility of wrongful convictions. Given his unshakeable trust in the justice system, I like to think that Kant would have demanded a higher threshold of evidence to convict a woman of infanticide than what was generally accepted as evidence in his day. But that question is bound to remain open.

Kant's views on marriage within this historical context allows for a better understanding of his shared concerns with other writers and highlights the innovative aspects of his account. We have also seen that the consequences of being excluded from the institution of marriage in eighteenth-century Germany were especially dire for the women accused of infanticide – an issue that Kant acknowledged and found important to address. But the issue of infanticide also illustrates that Kant's understanding of the equality of women is limited to the context of marriage rather than being grounded in a more substantial account of gender equality. This should make us wonder if Kant's account of marriage is delivering on its promises: what kind of rights and protection does it offer to those who enter it? And how helpful is the conception of equality it puts forward? I will now propose a closer analysis of how Kant views a certain form of spousal equality as the response to the threat posed by sexual objectification, and argue that to do that work effectively, his account of spousal equality must be grounded in a reform of women's status, guaranteeing them the same civil status as men's.

Many scholars have shown the interest of exploring the moral implications of marriage and sex within Kant's practical philosophy from a feminist perspective. Sexuality as Kant conceptualizes it in the *Metaphysics of Morals* raises several problems that his account of marriage intends to solve. It is notoriously unclear whether he succeeds or not: recent contributions have explored the implications of Kant's views on sexuality and investigated whether marriage can really achieve the purpose of making sexuality morally acceptable.[56] The egalitarian undertones of Kant's conception of marriage have also been frequently explored and questioned. Since Kant's conception of marriage requires a relative equality between men and women in order to fulfil its intended purpose, some commentators have suggested that his parallel commitment to the complementarity of men and women make his conception of marriage inconsistent from the start. While this view has been less popular in recent years, Okin (1982) and Pateman (1988) famously argue that Kant's conception of sexual difference stands in tension with his allegedly egalitarian conception of marriage.[57] Unlike Okin and Pateman, I do not take Kant's views on sexual

---

[56] Notably, Altman (2010); Beever (2013); Brake (2005); Denis (2001); Herman (1993); Papadaki (2007, 2010); Pascoe (2018); Sticker (2020); Varden (2017). Varden (2020) has also famously put forward a full-fledged Kantian theory of sex, love, and gender – moving away from his conception of freedom and rationality, and using instead some of his lesser-known insights on human nature, happiness and virtue as a steppingstone. Varden also explores the legal and political implications of her reconstructed account, always from a feminist and sex-positive approach. On Varden's account, there is thus enough material in Kant's practical philosophy that can be profitably used to reconcile his views with a more sex-positive approach, without needing to resort to marriage to make sex acceptable.

[57] Sticker (2020) pushes this point further by arguing that given Kant's views on the natural subordination of the wife to the husband, his account of marriage is more consistent if focused

difference to directly conflict with his account of marriage. Instead of regarding this account of marriage as flawed, I argue that we are justified, on the basis of Kant's account of marriage, in asking him for a more robust commitment to legal equality. In the *Doctrine of Right*, Kant argues for the legal subordination of women: as passive citizens, they are deprived of civil independence. However, his account of marriage would be considerably strengthened by granting equal civil status to men and women – which justifies revisiting his views on the legal subordination of women. In order to do so, I start by presenting Kant's account of sexual objectification and emphasizing why he sees it as a problem that can only be resolved through marriage. I then show how Kant intends marriage to be a moral safeguard for sexuality by drawing on an analogy he suggests between the concept of marriage and the concept of community put forward in the *Critique of Pure Reason*. Finally, I suggest that Kant's account of marriage would benefit from more egalitarian principles than those he put forward with respect to the civil status of women. If marriage is to secure a morally acceptable context for sexuality, it has to be through the reciprocity and legal equality of the partners. My argument draws on Kant's criticism of morganatic marriages, and shows that this criticism should be extended to any marriage in which the spouses have different civil status. This allows me to conclude that the civil subordination of women put forward in Kant's *Doctrine of Right* should be questioned and revisited on the basis of his own account of marriage, thus showing that Kant is offering us compelling reasons to embrace a conception of gender equality that reaches beyond marriage (like Hippel, for instance, was suggesting) – instead of limiting it to a specific form of spousal equality like he intended to.

Sex and Objectification

When investigating Kant's account of sexuality, one must acknowledge that Kant is working with certain assumptions that we may well not share – the most egregious one being that sexual intercourse should only occur between a man and a woman, which I have more extensively discussed in the second section of

---

on same-sex marriage. I agree that Kant's claims on sexual difference (and on the political subordination he takes them to suggest) stand in tension with his egalitarian account of marriage. But while Sticker offers a plausible argument to rehabilitate same-sex marriage from a Kantian perspective, his conclusion (that Kant's views on marriage ultimately make more sense when applied to same-sex marriage than to heterosexual marriage) strikes me as moving Kant's ideas in a different (and innovative) direction. Ultimately, Stickler's project, like Altman's or Varden's, is doing a very important type of work: Shedding light on the transformative possibilities of a Kantian account of marriage in light of contemporary issues – regardless of whether Kant would have been able to embrace these critical appropriations or not. My project here is a bit different, and consists primarily in shedding light on the conception of equality required by Kant's account of marriage, in dialogue with other writers from his time.

this Element. Another important and controversial assumption grounding Kant's conception of sexuality is that sexuality raises a challenge for morality that other enjoyable activities do not. This assumption is more thoroughly justified than the first one and sets the grounds for Kant's criticism of the objectification process at stake in sex. Sexual pleasure as Kant understands it is relational in nature: it is pleasure obtained "from the enjoyment of another person" (MM 6: 426). This key element is also taken up in Kant's definition of sexual activity:

> Sexual union (*commercium sexuale*) is the reciprocal use that one human being makes of the sexual organs and capacities of another. (MM 6: 277)

In characterizing sexuality as interpersonal, Kant makes clear that the problem specifically associated with sexual desire has something to do with the fact that it requires the enjoyment, not of a good meal or of a movie, but of another human being. This constitutes a good entry point to his account of objectification.[58] The objectification at work in sex is twofold: there is one's own objectification, but also the objectification of one's sexual partner. While Kant tends to focus more on the damages one inflicts to oneself by engaging in sexual activity than on the damages one inflicts to their sexual partner, both aspects can be criticized on similar grounds. A closer look at Kant's depiction of sex allows for a better understanding of the problem at stake:

> In [giving himself to the other], a human being makes himself into a thing, which conflicts with the Right of humanity in his own person. (MM 6: 278)

The Right of humanity is defined as the possession of "[f]reedom (independence from being constrained by another's choice), insofar as it can coexist with the freedom of every other in accordance with a universal law" (MM 6: 237). It is a right that belongs to us by virtue of our humanity. Making oneself into a thing directly conflicts with that right, because as a thing, one is deprived of freedom. This also echoes the well-known formula of humanity of the categorical imperative: "So act that you use humanity, in your own person as well as in the person of any other, always at the same time as an end, never merely as a means" (G 4: 429).

The formula of humanity, by reminding us to treat our own person *as well as the person of any other* always at the same time as an end and never merely as

---

[58] Kant himself does not use the word "objectification": When referring to the problem he associates with sexuality, he generally says that human beings are making themselves or others into things. The term "objectification" has, since then, been coined to refer to this phenomenon – within Kantian scholarship (by Herman (1993), Papadaki (2007, 2010), and others), but also, more broadly, in ethics and in feminist theory.

a means, suggests that what raises an issue for oneself in sexuality will also raise an issue for others. Turning others into things, or using them as mere means, is just as problematic as turning oneself into a thing, or using oneself as a mere means. The formula of humanity commands different duties (to oneself and to others), but those duties are grounded in one and the same issue: not treating humanity (in oneself or in others) as a thing. This justifies extending Kant's conception of objectification to the objectification of others.

But we have yet to understand how this objectification takes place. It is tempting to assume that any kind of use of another person's body (or of our own), broadly speaking, may result in using that person as a mere means – and that this is why sexuality is so dangerous. This is partly Kant's fault, as he sometimes seems to imply that what is problematic in sexuality is that it involves one's own body or someone else's body. But there are plenty of ways in which we may use other people's bodies: for instance, when we hire a carpenter to build furniture, when a couple of ballet dancers use each other's bodies to perform complex figures, or when Leonardo da Vinci painted Lisa Gherardini's portrait. Yet it is not clear that the bodies being used in those examples are being enjoyed in a way that turns the person they belong to into a thing. Using someone else's body may be using that person as a means, but it does not imply that we are using the person merely as a means – that is that we are thereby disregarding his or her humanity. Kant makes this distinction clear in his lectures on ethics: "Man can certainly enjoy the other as an instrument for his service; he can utilize the others' hands or feet to serve him, though by the latter's free choice. But we never find that a human being can be the object of another's enjoyment, save through the sexual impulse." (L-Eth Collins 27: 384) Using the hands of a carpenter to perform work he or she has agreed to perform, or the body of a dance partner to perform a couple's dance, thus seem like uncontroversial uses of other people's bodies to serve certain ends that do not disregard the humanity of the persons being used – as the bodies involved are not themselves objects of enjoyment. The case of the model used for a painting is less straightforward, as here the body does seem to be used as an object of enjoyment, broadly construed – but without being the object of another person's appetite.[59] Despite Kant's general disdain of bodily pleasures, objectification cannot be reduced to any kind of use of one's own body or of other people's bodies. So while using and enjoying other people's bodies is definitely part of the problem, it does not entirely explain what's wrong with sex.

Kant's answer turns out to be simple – perhaps too simple: sexual desire is inherently objectifying, in a way in which the urge to dance or to paint the

---

[59] Similarly, Brake notes that a chess player can be valued as a good opponent, without thereby turning him or her into an object of appetite: strictly speaking, the game is the object of appetite, not the player (Brake 2005, 67).

portrait of a beautiful model is not.⁶⁰ Sexual desire as he sees it turns out to be an inclination not for another human being as a whole, but rather for the body of that person only, making them the object of our appetite, as confirmed in the following passages from the Collins lectures on ethics:

(i) In loving from sexual inclination, [we] make the person into an object of their appetite. As soon as the person is possessed, and the appetite sated, they are thrown away, as one throws away a lemon after sucking the juice from it (L-Eth 27: 384).
(ii) [...] the sexual impulse is not an inclination that one human has for another, *qua* human, but an inclination for their sex [...] (L-Eth 27: 385)
(iii) [...] for as soon as anyone becomes an object of another's appetite, all motives of moral relationship fall away; as object of the other's appetite, that person is in fact a thing, whereby the other's appetite is sated, and can be misused as such a thing by anybody (L-Eth 27: 384–385).

The main ethical problem associated with sex is that it involves the fragmentation of the self: in engaging in sexual activity and through sexual desire, we offer ourselves as a mere body, or even, as emphasized in passage (ii), as mere sex organs, to the other's sexual appetite, thereby turning ourselves into a thing and ignoring our humanity. And we're similarly disregarding our partner's humanity. This problem points back to Kant's distinction between a person and a thing. A person is "a subject whose actions can be imputed to him," while a thing lacks freedom: it is "an object of free choice which itself lacks freedom (*res corporalis*)," to which nothing can be imputed (MM 6: 223). As persons, we are both sensible and intelligible beings. A person is "an absolute unity" (MM 6: 278). No part of the person (body or mind) can be dismissed. Because of this indivisibility, one does not have the right to dispose of their own body, and not even of some body part – as all our body parts are an intrinsic part of our person. The absolute unity or indivisibility of the person implies that our body is not quite like some kind of property that we can divide as we please.⁶¹ It also implies that whenever we treat ourselves as a mere body (or as a mere mind), we also disregard part of our person.

---

⁶⁰ Williams notes that premise is contentious. While it is by no means self-evident, it can be partly explained by the increased involvement of capitalism in the economic and social life at the time (Williams 1983, 117–118).
⁶¹ This is not to say that no analogies can be made between body and property: Pascoe demonstrates that Kant captures sexual access in terms of property right rather than contract right, which is especially helpful to make sense of his criticism of sex work (Pascoe 2022, 21–22). But there are limits to this analogy, as our body is not something that can be divided as we please, even when we are its rightful owner. Kant condemns organ donation on these grounds in MM 6: 423.

Sexuality thus involves a problematic twofold objectification – that of the seducer and that of the seduced, to use Beever's characterization (2013, 343). In engaging in sexual activity, we offer ourselves as a mere body to the other, thereby disregarding the rest of our personhood. But that's not the only problem associated with sexuality – as we also have duties of respect to others. Those duties to others are easier to enforce through external, juridical laws – the focus of Kant's *Doctrine of Right*, and the very reason marriage comes into play. But even from a strictly ethical perspective, enjoying the body of another person while disregarding the rest of their personhood is no different than using them as a mere means, as a thing, to satisfy our own pleasure. We are therefore doubly compromising humanity: in our person, and in the person of our sexual partner.

The idea that people turn themselves and each other into things when they have sex is of course a strong assumption to work with. Kant does not further explain why sexual desire necessarily results in objectification. I have provided so far a way to make sense of what he may find unique about sexual desire. But Kant's claim about objectification can still come across as odd. It is worth noting, following Herman's influential article, that the twofold objectification process at work in Kant's conception of sexuality can be connected to some fundamental insights of radical feminism (Herman 1993, 61 sq.).[62] As noted by Herman, for Andrea Dworkin just like for Kant, the process of objectification is twofold. Women are objectified by men through intercourse, but also take part in their own objectification by embracing their object status. A woman who engages in sexual intercourse is simultaneously turning herself into an object and being objectified by her partner. This does not mean that Kant had a direct influence on her ideas.[63] But it at least suggests that Kant's assumption is more widely shared than thought – and is certainly worth reflecting on. Contemporary essays in feminist philosophy still engage with conceptions of objectification

---

[62] Dworkin's criticism of heterosexual sexuality proves to be particularly interesting in that respect, as Dworkin associates sexual intercourse with an objectification process – and with the objectification of women in particular. Herman notes obvious limits to her parallel, starting with the fact that Kant's conception of sexuality shows no particular concern for the objectification of women (all partners being equally objectified) (Herman 1993, 56). Williams also notes this disanalogy between Kant's account of sexual objectification and feminist arguments like Dworkin's, stressing that sex, for Kant, is best understood as revealing "the general inhumanity of man (i.e. human beings in general) towards man" (1983, 118).

[63] Wood (1999) discusses the possible indirect influence of Kant's views on objectification on Dworkin through Jean-Paul Sartre and Simone de Beauvoir: "There is little in Dworkin that was not anticipated by Simone de Beauvoir, who is quite often condescended to by contemporary feminists, though not nearly as often as they make use of her ideas without acknowledgment [...]. Beauvoir's discussion of sex is in turn dependent on Jean-Paul Sartre, who took over Kant's view of sex with mainly terminological and stylistic modifications" (Wood 1999, 396–397 n11). We can add to Wood's reflection that Beauvoir's influence is also noticeable in Shulamith Firestone's *The Dialectic of Sex: The Case for Feminist Revolution* (1970), who in turn influenced Dworkin's *Woman Hating: A Radical Look at Sexuality* (1974).

that are influenced (directly or indirectly) by Kantian insights. An excellent example is Manon Garcia's 2023 monograph *The Joy of Consent: A Philosophy of Good Sex*, which contrasts and analyzes the implications of different conceptions of sexual consent. One of the conceptions put forward and reviewed by Garcia is informed by Kantian insights on sexuality and dignity. Garcia argues that if one is to embrace this Kantian form of consent, consent cannot simply consist in formally agreeing to something: it also should set more demanding conditions for the agreement to happen, so that the humanity and dignity of the parties involved are preserved.[64]

If we take seriously the threat of objectification raised by sexuality, we can see that it calls for a robust solution. Because sexual desire is inherently objectifying, giving consent to having sex cannot possibly cancel out the objectification process, so long as consent is understood in its usual "formal agreement" sense (as opposed to the more demanding sense that Garcia is putting forward). This is not to say that consent, understood as formal assent, is irrelevant by Kant's standards: violating someone's consent would be an infringement of their innate right to freedom, that is "[the] independence from being constrained by another's choice insofar as it can coexist with the freedom of every other in accordance with a universal law" (MM 6: 237). This innate right belongs to every human being by virtue of their humanity.[65] But while consent is of foremost importance to Kant's conception of sexuality and freedom in general, it nevertheless fails to address the objectification process at stake in sexual intercourse. Dworkin's analysis of heterosexual sexuality points to a similar problem: women's consent does not put an end to the objectification at work – by giving consent, women are in fact collaborating in their own objectification. Similarly, in a Kantian perspective, one could argue that giving consent to having sex, as if sexuality were a contract, makes sense only insofar as we are persons, that is moral agents. But since sex turns us into things, it simultaneously makes our consent invalid – as the consent is not provided by a person anymore. Beever suggests a parallel with slavery to better illustrate this point: one cannot give

---

[64] Varden's monograph *Sex, Love, and Gender: A Kantian Theory* is also an excellent example of this trend, as the volume explores how certain neglected Kantian insights (notably on human nature and animality) can contribute to a better understanding of what, exactly, leads to problematic forms of objectification in sex (Varden 2020, especially 123 sq.).

[65] It has been noted that Kant remains shockingly quiet regarding whether marital rape is permissible or not, as he brings up the topic in a casuistical question: "If, for example, [... the wife] feels no desire for intercourse, is it not contrary to nature's end, and so also contrary to one's duty to oneself, for one or the other of them, to make use of their sexual attributes – just as in unnatural lust?" (MM 6: 426) While my understanding is that Kant leaves the question unanswered, Mertens interprets his silence to indicate that he endorses marital rape (Mertens 2014, 338). Brake, while acknowledging the awkwardness of Kant's silence, notes that such endorsement would clearly contradict the freedom that marriage is intended to protect (Brake 2005, 90n10). Varden, then, pushes this view further by arguing that Kant's account "recognizes marital rape as a criminal act" (Varden 2020, 254).

consent to making oneself property because it would make one both person and non-person (thing) at the same time (2013, 350–351). A similar issue is raised by the idea of consensual cannibalism.[66] In a Kantian framework, unmarried sex, just like slavery and cannibalism, implies giving away something that we do not have the right to give up on our dignity as a person. By Kant's standards, I can consent to partake in a football game or to sell my labour-power in exchange for a salary without thereby giving away my autonomy as a person. But I cannot consent to something that would imply giving up on what makes me a human being, which, for him, is the case of sex. Kant's worries about sexuality thus require a solution that goes beyond sexual consent in the sense we normally understand it – marriage.

Community

Despite the dangers he associates with sexuality, Kant believes it can be desirable in some contexts. First and foremost, because of the obvious role of sexuality in procreation. But as we have seen earlier, sexuality need not be restricted to that role, even by his standards. The question is, then, how to provide a context within which the partners can enjoy the benefits of sexuality without at the same time compromising humanity in their person and in that of their partner. As we will now see, the external constraint provided by the institution of marriage seems to be the best way to address the issue at stake. I will now put forward an interpretation of Kant's account of marriage based on the analogy he suggests between marriage and the category of community previously introduced in the *Critique of Pure Reason*. This should provide a better understanding of the role of marriage by clarifying the nature of the relationship between the spouses.

Kant comes up with a robust account of marriage that requires the creation of a new legal category: the "rights to persons akin to rights to things" (MM 6: 276 sq.).[67] It has no equivalent in any of his main sources on natural law.[68] The unique kind of right this category puts forward is meant to provide

---

[66] Like the highly mediatized case of Armin Meiwes and Bernd Jürgen Brandes, where Brandes consented to be killed and eaten by Meiwes. The latter's consent to being killed and eaten seems to have made a difference in Meiwes' sentence – as he was originally charged with manslaughter rather than with murder. Meiwes now self-describes as an environmentalist who grew increasingly critical of factory farming, and has allegedly embraced a vegetarian diet in prison – which, if true, seems to indicate that consent matters to him, although perhaps not consent in the more substantial Kantian sense put forward by Garcia. I thank Louise Daoust for bringing this case to my attention.

[67] This legal category was quite innovative in Kant's day and was then called a "new phenomenon in the juristic sky" – see Bouterwek's 1798 review of the *Doctrine of Right* to which Kant refers in his later Appendix to the Doctrine of Right (MM 6: 356 sq.) It is, however, not clear whether Kant's new legal conception of marriage had influence on subsequent accounts. J.G. Fichte, for instance, returns to a contractual conception of marriage.

[68] For instance in G. Achenwall's *Jus Naturae*; S. Pufendorf's *De Jure Naturae et Gentium*. But beyond this new legal category, Kant's general conception of marriage is likely indebted to the

an alternative to property right and contract right that borrows from both traditions without being limited to one or the other. It is at the core of Kant's account of domestic right, and as such, is intended to make sense not only of the rights and obligations of spouses towards one another but also of parental right, as well as of the relationship between servants and the head of the household. For my purposes here, I will pay special attention to the ways in which this legal category grounds the possibility for spouses to enjoy sex in a safe(r) context.

The concept of possession is essential to understanding Kant's account of domestic right. The concept of private right in general involves the claim that something external to me is mine. And what makes it possible for me to use something that is rightfully mine is that I have it in my possession. Kant uses the concept of possession in an intelligible sense: the possession at stake does not have to be an object that one is physically holding. There are three possible kinds of objects of possession:

(i) A corporeal thing external to me (the object of property right)
(ii) Another's choice to perform a specific deed (the object of contract right)
(iii) Another's status in relation to me (the object of the "right to a person akin to a right to a thing") (MM 6: 247)

Kant's new legal category applies to the third kind of object. "Property" can only refer to things, never to persons (MM 6: 359), as treating someone else or our own person as a thing would do wrong to humanity in the person of others or in our own person.[69] Property right thus cannot be directly applied to persons. While our right on our spouse is in some ways "akin to a right to a thing,"[70] this right must take into account that we are dealing with another free, rational being – with whom we stand in a moral relation and towards whom we have duties. The possession of a spouse is therefore not the result of a unilateral acquisition like property, that is, a legal deed made by a person involving an object that has no say in the decision.

The 1798 Appendix to the *Doctrine of Right*, in response to a concern raised by Bouterwek in his review, attempts to further distinguish between the

---

German School of Natural Law and possibly also to the ideas of the French jurist Charles Dumoulin (*Tractatus commerciorum et usurarum, redituumque pecunia constitutorum et monetarum*, 1546), who also compares marriage to a community. On the legal sources of Kant's conception of marriage, see Goyard-Fabre 1996, 136–137.

[69] This also holds for oneself: One can be their own master (*sui iuris*), but strictly speaking, one cannot be the owner of themselves (*sui dominus*) (MM 6: 270).

[70] In that each partner has certain rights over the other: One person cannot simply leave the marriage as he or she wants (MM 6: 278).

possession of a spouse and the possession of an object of property by comparing the former to usufruct (*ius utendi fruendi*). Kant makes the following claim:

> What is one's own here does not, indeed, mean what is one's own in the sense of property in the person of another (for a human being cannot have property in himself, much less in another person), <u>but means what is one's own in the sense of usufruct (*ius utendi fruendi*)</u>, to make direct use of a person *as of a thing, as a means to my end*, but still without infringing upon his personality. (MM 6: 359; emphasis mine)

The analogy between spouse and usufruct is helpful in that it emphasizes that even though spouse A acquired spouse B through marriage, spouse A only has use of spouse B in a limited and nonsubstantial sense. The analogy also has its limits: in Roman civil law, usufruct still implies a reference to property, as it refers to the right to use *someone else's* property. This implies that each spouse has property in themselves (even if the other spouse does not), which goes against what Kant says in MM 6: 270: "[...] a man can be his own master (*sui iuris*) but cannot be the owner of himself (*sui dominus*) (cannot dispose of himself as he pleases) – still less can he dispose of other men as he pleases – since he is accountable to the humanity in his own person" (MM 6: 270).[71]

But Kant's account of marriage, despite being often referred to as contractual, also differs from legal contracts. Marriage bears some similarity with contract right: due to the interpersonal relation it involves, it has more to do, in certain ways, with the united choice of two persons grounding a contract than with the unilateral choice grounding property acquisition. But a contract, strictly speaking, involves a person's performance, not the person himself or herself – whereas marriage involves the spouses themselves in a very important way, in that they possess each other. This is where the concept of community can contribute to clarifying the unique form of relationship grounding marriage.

It is not unusual for Kant to use the concept of community [*Gemeinschaft*] in his political philosophy – for instance, when referring to the community of peoples grounding cosmopolitanism: "The growing prevalence of a (narrower or wider) community among the peoples of the earth has now reached a point at which the violation of right at any one place on the earth is felt in all places" (TPP 8: 360).

While the connection between this form of cosmopolitan community and the pure concept of community put forward in the *Critique of Pure Reason* is not further discussed, Kant further clarifies the difference between contract right

---

[71] On this topic, see also the Vigilantius lecture notes (L-Eth 27:593 sq.) Kant's account of possession and the distinction between property and usufruct are also further analyzed in K. R. Westphal's "Do Kant's Principles Justify Property or Usufruct?" (1997).

and marriage by explicitly associating the former to the category of causality and the latter to the category of community (MM 6: 247, 276). A contract involves a linear, causal relationship, taking place over a certain period of time. If I work as a snow shoveler, sign a contract with customers and shovel snow for X hours, I will then get a certain amount of money for my work. My salary is thus conditional to my work.

But marriage, like parenting and like the relationship between head of the household and servants, does not rely on a linear causal relation so much as on the relation at stake in a community: all parts involved mutually influence one another. Kant distinguishes between those two categories in the *Critique of Pure Reason* by pointing out that in causality, the consequence "does not reciprocally determine the ground and therefore does not constitute a whole with the latter" (B112). Causality implies that one of the things involved (the effect) is subordinated under the other (the cause), and conditioned by it. Community, on the other hand, requires that each thing involved be coordinated with the other simultaneously and reciprocally – each one being the cause of the determination of the other:

> [In the category of community,] a similar connection is thought of in an entirety of things, since one is not subordinated, as effect, under another, as the cause of its existence, but is rather coordinated with the other simultaneously and reciprocally as cause with regard to its determination (e.g., in a body, the parts of which reciprocally attract yet also repel each other), [...] (B112)

The concept of community makes sense of the relationship between parts of a whole that are not subordinated to one another in a causal manner. They stand in a reciprocal relationship and are all contributing to the whole in an equal manner – just like body parts. The concept of community proves useful in making sense of Kant's conception of marriage as a legal relationship that is taking place in a reciprocal and simultaneous manner. The spouses' possession of each other is therefore not conditional to something else in a contractual manner. The *Doctrine of Right* provides a few definitions of marriage:

(i) Sexual union in accordance with principle [rather than with mere animal nature] is *marriage* (*matrimonium*), that is, the union of two persons of different sexes for lifelong possession of each other's sexual attributes (MM 6: 277).
(ii) [M]arriage is a reciprocal giving of one's very person into the possession of the other (MM 6: 359)
(iii) In [giving himself to the other], a human being makes himself into a thing, which conflicts with the Right of humanity in his own person. There is

only one condition under which this is possible: that while one person is acquired by the other *as if it were a thing*, the one who is acquired acquires the other in turn; for this way each reclaims itself and restores its personality (MM 6: 278).

In these three passages, Kant consistently describes marriage as implying the reciprocal possession of the spouses. He is less consistent in describing what that possession entails: passage (i) emphasizes the "sexual attributes," while passage (ii) emphasizes the "very person." Kant is similarly inconsistent in describing the problem at stake in sexual desire: he sometimes suggests that the problem is to desire the other person as a mere body, and sometimes suggests that the problem is to desire the other person only for their sexual attributes. Considering the absolute unity and indivisibility of the person emphasized earlier, both formulations point to the same problem: what is at stake is the idea of disregarding the full personhood of sexual partners (by focusing either just on their sexual attributes, or even on their entire body – always at the expense of the rest of their person). So while passage (i) probably insists on the sexual attributes because of the nature of the discussion, it seems preferable to describe marriage as in passages (ii) and (iii), that is as the possession of the person as a whole.

A marriage is thus a unique form of legal bond with another person. Such relationship entails a complete equality of possession under the law, including the possession of the partners themselves as well as that of their material goods and properties. Each partner thus acquires the other as a whole – including material goods, but also body and mind. The reciprocity aspect is very important: by mutually acquiring each other, the partners not only acquire each other, but also acquire themselves back through the other who acquired them. Since all of this is happening simultaneously, marriage can be understood in light of certain aspects of the concept of community put forward in the first *Critique*. The husband and the wife are each, so to speak, the ground of the determination of the other: without the wife, there is no husband, and without the husband, there is no wife. They mutually contribute to a common end: to the community that they together constitute.

And yet we can wonder whether Kant's conception of marriage really succeeds in solving the moral problem associated with sexuality. The core idea is promising: within marriage, both partners acquire each other's full person (and not merely their body), which makes them equally and reciprocally committed to the other as a whole person. That's certainly an effective moral safeguard in that it prevents some of the harmful consequences Kant associates with sex. But Kant's solution remains incomplete in two ways. First, his account of marriage does not entirely clarify how the mutual acquisition of the spouses overcomes the objectification process associated with sexuality. Second, Kant's account of marriage does not clarify to what extent the relationship between the spouses must be a reciprocal one, nor what the implications of this reciprocity are for his conception of sexual difference.

The first problem has been amply discussed in the secondary literature: Kant does not further explain how marriage can avoid or overcome the objectification caused by sexual activity. If my body and my person are unalienable and that sex involves the mutual objectification of the partners, it is hard to see how any kind of legal procedure or institution would render this objectification acceptable. This part of Kant's solution thus requires further explanation, which is not the main aim of this discussion. I will briefly describe some of the most interesting proposals made in that respect before moving on to the second problem, that of the legal equality required for marriage.

Kant seems to understand marriage as rendering sex acceptable insofar as it provides special legal circumstances under which the objectification process is altered and removed. These special circumstances have been understood in (at least) two main ways in the secondary literature.[72] First, as a legally binding exchange in which each partner, while mutually giving themselves to each other, simultaneously acquire themselves back.[73] This is corroborated by the description of marriage in passage (iii) from the *Doctrine of Right*:

> There is only one condition under which [it] is possible [to give oneself to another]: that while one person is acquired by the other *as if it were a thing*, the one who is acquired acquires the other in turn; for this way each reclaims itself and restores its personality. (MM 6: 278)

What Kant seems to have in mind here is that if spouses acquire each other through marriage, and thereby possess not only the other but also themselves through the other, they can engage in marital sex without dehumanizing themselves or their partner. More precisely, they still give themselves away but are at the same time always already getting themselves back since spouses mutually possess each other in marriage. In simultaneously giving themselves to each other, they in fact never lose possession of themselves. Whatever use they make of each other's body in this

---

[72] Other commentators have rejected Kant's solution altogether. Brake (2005), while acknowledging the relevance of Kant's views on sex for contemporary feminist theory, rejects the legal dimension of his solution to objectification as misguided: The pitfall of sex is in a failure in virtue, not a violation of rights. The objectification associated with sexuality can thus only be avoided on the grounds of virtue – if one manages to develop a particular sentiment of respect towards their partner.

[73] Different versions of this interpretation have been developed by Altman (2011); Denis (2001); Herman (1993), who ultimately rejects this possibility in favour of the next one; Mertens (2014); and Papadaki (2007, 2010).

unique legal context is thus no different than the use they make of their own body. This interpretation culminates in the idea of a "unity of will" between spouses mentioned in Kant's lectures on ethics (L-Eth Collins 27: 388). The married couple becomes something like a bigger moral entity, in the manner of a state. This explanation further reinforces the importance of Kant's reference to the category of community: this unity is made possible by the simultaneity and reciprocity of the relationship between spouses. In the end, this interpretation is helpful in many ways but still does not explain how forming a marital community overcomes the objectification caused by sex. To be sure, the threat of coercion implied in this unique legal arrangement manages to constraint the spouses to "act in ways that respect the person [of each other], at least outwardly," as noted by Altman (2011, 320). But we have seen earlier that engaging in sex results in a twofold objectification: that of the other and that of oneself. So even if the first one was resolved through this novel arrangement, the objectification of oneself would still occur.

If sexual desire is inherently objectifying, we are left with two options: either Kant's conception of marriage does not fulfill its goal, or it does so by modifying the nature of sexual desire. This is the spirit of the second proposed solution to the problem of objectification, first put forward by Herman, later embraced to some degree by Varden as compatible with her own reading (Varden 2020, 123 sq.), and echoed by Pascoe's different but parallel solution, also focusing on the transformative role of legal institutions (more specifically, on the transformative role of domestic right on external freedom; Pascoe 2011, 22). These proposals all attempt to acknowledge the significance of the change occurring within a legal context like that of marriage, thus confirming its role as a transformative institution. Herman argues that the legal institutions put forward in the *Doctrine of Right* (and marriage in this case) can contribute to shape our moral regard and thus change the way we think of sexuality (Herman 1993, 57 sq.) Marriage would thus reverse the objectification process normally present in sexual desire. Just like the first proposal, this solution requires the reciprocity between spouses made possible by the community-like nature of their relationship.[74]

Citizenship and Subordination

The problem raised by the objectification tied into sexual desire is one that I will leave aside for the rest of this investigation. But whether we agree with Kant that his account of marriage provides an effective moral safeguard for sex or that we

---

[74] While Herman's resolution is plausible, it runs into another issue: Kant regards sexuality first and foremost as a natural impulse – which is hard to reconcile with a socially constructed account of sexual desire. So while this proposal likely offers the best answer to the question as to how marriage makes sexuality acceptable, it seems unlikely that Kant himself had this solution in mind.

argue that it requires further adjustments, it seems like his solution also requires a more robust commitment to the legal equality of men and women, as I will now show. The rest of this section thus turns to the second problem: figuring out how to reconcile the reciprocity between spouses with Kant's conception of sexual difference. I will now argue that by limiting his conception of gender equality to the strict framework of marriage, Kant in fact weakens his own argument: the subordinated civil status of women becomes an important obstacle to the reciprocity grounding Kant's account of marriage. Getting rid of the legal subordination of women thus makes his account of marriage stronger and more consistent.

Kant, still in the *Doctrine of Right*, puts forward his own conception of citizenship and, following the Abbé Sieyès, distinguishes between active and passive citizens. It is worth recalling the passage in which that distinction is introduced:

> This quality of being independent [...] requires a distinction between active and passive citizens, though the concept of passive citizen seems to contradict the concept of a citizen as such. The following examples can serve to remove this difficulty: an apprentice in the service of a merchant or artisan; a domestic servant [...]; a minor [...]; all women and, in general, anyone whose preservation in existence (his being fed and protected) depends not on his management of his own business but on arrangements made by another. (MM 6: 314)

Kant's conception of active citizenship is thus based on civil independence, meaning that only the active citizen is entitled to represent himself when it comes to legal matters. Passive citizens are "under the direction or protection of other individuals" (MM 6: 315) and do not have civil independence. They do not get to take an active part in public affairs either.[75] We should also keep in mind that, still according to Kant's categories of citizenship, women differ from other passive citizens. While he is, in principle, open to social mobility and argues that passive citizens should be able to work their way up to active citizenship, he nevertheless claims that in order to be an active citizen and to take part in public affairs, one must be a man (TP 8: 295). Women thus seem to be confined to passive citizenship.

The problem posed by the peculiar civil status of women for Kant's conception of marriage has already been noted. Pateman's argument, for instance, goes as follows: if marriage involves a legal acquisition and if women, due to their lack of civil personality, cannot take part in public affairs, it seems like only men

---

[75] Williams (2006) investigates the importance of independence in Kant's political philosophy, and emphasizes the restrictions that are built in this ideal.

are really performing the acquisition at stake, for they are the only ones who can enter into contracts (1988). Similar concerns have been raised by Okin (1982). Wilson has responded to Pateman by pointing out that women are not the only passive citizens, and that surely Kant allows for domestic servants and other passive citizens to perform some basic legal acts like getting married (2004). Wilson's point is fair, although it conceals an important issue: the fact that many servants (men or women) were, in fact, not allowed to enter marriage in Kant's day, with the consequences we know. But I nevertheless believe that the peculiar status of women or, at the very least, Kant's insistence in confining them to passive citizenship, stands in tension with his account of marriage.[76]

It is interesting to note that Kant himself wondered whether sexual difference could threaten the legal equality of the spouses required for marriage:

> If the question is therefore posed, whether it is also in conflict with the equality of the partners for the law to say of the husband's relation to the wife, he is to be your master [. . .]: This cannot be regarded as conflicting with the natural equality of a couple if this dominance is based only on the natural superiority of the husband to the wife in his capacity to promote the common interest of the household, and the right to direct that is based on this can be derived from the very duty of unity and equality with respect to the *end*. (MM 6: 279)

Here, Kant explicitly acknowledges that the natural equality of a couple grounding marriage could be threatened by some inequalities – yet not by those he regards as natural inequalities – when he says that "This cannot be regarded as conflicting with the natural equality of a couple *if* this dominance is based only on the natural superiority of the husband's relation . . ." Kant's conception of marriage is far from being completely egalitarian: just like it does not question the distribution of labour in the household, for instance, it also leaves untouched his questionable anthropological assumptions about the complementarity of the sexes.[77] Just like he believes that the woman *refuses* and the man *woos*, Kant

---

[76] This issue is well summarized by Wood, as he points out that "we cannot help asking how far exclusive possession of her husband's sexual capacities could really go toward protecting a woman's personality as long as she remained economically dependent on him and her life-activities were confined by both law and custom to the domestic sphere." (Wood 1999, 259) I also believe that an extra step is required for Kant's account of marriage to perform the work he is expecting it to.

[77] Denis shows that these assumptions are not necessary for Kant's account (2001, 19). Yet they do not conflict with it either: Kant's account of marriage requires a certain form of equality, but not the sameness of the partners (unlike Sticker's critical appropriation of Kant's account, which seems to require sameness). The fact that Kant's new category of right applies not only to married couples, but also to families and to the whole household, shows that the analogy between marriage (or family, or household) and community does not entail that every member of the community is qualitatively identical or equal to the other in every respect. Kant's own way of illustrating the analogy of community in the first *Critique* is by referring to body parts that

believes that within marriage "the woman should *dominate* and the husband should *govern*; for inclination dominates, and understanding governs." (Anth 7: 306, 309). Yet on the legal level, any marriage must be egalitarian. And Kant seems to acknowledge that some forms of inequality could threaten the egalitarian grounds of marriage. In fact, he even gives an example where marriage cannot be the moral safeguard it is meant to be: the case of morganatic marriages.

Morganatic marriages (*Ehe an der linken Hand*: literally, "left-hand marriage") refer to unions between people of unequal social ranks where one of the spouses is denied the privileges, rights or properties of the other. While the practice was not very common in eighteenth-century Germany, it was definitely well known. Kant objects to morganatic marriages on rather interesting grounds:

> [A morganatic marriage] takes advantage of the inequality of Estate of the two parties to give one of them domination over the other; for in fact morganatic marriage is not different, in terms of natural Right only, from concubinage and is no true marriage. (MM 6: 279)[78]

One of Kant's reasons for objecting to morganatic marriages is not mentioned in this passage, but pertains to his general disapproval of hereditary nobility, which he regards as "a rank that precedes merit and also provides no basis to hope for merit" (MM 6: 329). Morganatic marriages further emphasize the arbitrariness of hereditary nobility, as the rank of one of the spouses (typically, the husband) is not passed on to the other spouse nor to their children. But Kant objects to morganatic marriages not only because the rank of one of the spouses is not extended to the other, but also because other possessions (in a legal sense) remain separate. This aspect is emphasized in Kant's lectures on ethics:

> [A] morganatic marriage does not fully accord with the right of humanity. For the wife is not in possession of all the husband's rights, and so does not have total possession of him, though he has absolute disposition over her. (L-Eth Vigilantius 27: 641)

Here, Kant extends his reasoning to the rights that are not shared amongst the spouses, thereby confirming that marriage should entail a complete sharing of possessions. The example of morganatic marriages shows that Kant is aware

---

mutually influence each other – this mutual influence and reciprocity does not entail that the body parts are qualitatively identical to each other. However, his anthropological assumptions can be easily challenged on different grounds – for instance, by questioning the reliability of his empirical observations about women. Varden's 2020 monograph questions the ways in which Kant's own bias may have shaped his observations, and advocates that it provides us with resources to overcome them.

[78] See also, in Kant's lectures on ethics, L-Eth *Vigilantius* 27: 641.

that significant differences in political power between the spouses can compromise the role that marriage is intended to play. Through marriage, each spouse acquires the other person as a whole. This is the only context in which we have seen sex becomes morally acceptable. But in morganatic marriages, one of the partners has legal domination over the other, which compromises the reciprocity grounding marriage.[79] I believe that this reasoning should be extended to men and women's civil status. While it is of course possible for an active citizen to share all of his belongings with his wife (who is de facto a passive citizen), there will always remain a significant difference between the two with respect to their ability to take part in public affairs that may be relevant for the household. Men's civil status, and the rights and privileges that come with it, cannot be extended to their wives. One of the partners is thus effectively subordinated to the other on the legal level. This discrepancy, in light of Kant's reservations towards morganatic marriages, provides reasonable grounds for asking Kant's practical philosophy to do a little more work towards gender equality. Within the *Doctrine of Right*, the only type of marriage that would meet the legal equality criterion would be that of passive citizens, such as servants – which provides grounds to revisit the civil status of women on his behalf. Kant's conception of spousal equality thus strikes me as too narrow on its own to achieve the role he intended for it, which emphasizes the importance of operating broader reforms in society – like Hippel, for instance, suggested. Ensuring an equal civil status to men and women seems like a necessary step in securing the equality and reciprocity that Kant visibly cared about, and wanted spouses to enjoy.

5 Concluding Remarks

In this Element, I have investigated the feminist implications and limitations of Kant's account of marriage by paying special attention to its entanglement with broader legal and political discourses of eighteenth-century Germany. I hope to have done justice to the radicality of Kant's thoughts as much as to the complexity of his interactions with his contemporaries. The purpose of marriage

---

[79] Sticker's argument runs parallel to mine, in that he also notes that Kant's criticism of morganatic marriages should commit him to the claim that partners ought to be legally equal. However, Sticker is interested in different implications of that claim: For him, the requirement of legal equality we may infer from Kant's criticism ultimately justifies the idea that only partners who share equal civil status may enter marriage – thus making same-sex marriage the only legitimate form of marriage. (Sticker 2020, 450). Pascoe, on the other hand, emphasizes the limits of Kant's criticism of morganatic marriage. While a certain level of legal equality is required within marriage, and that morganatic marriage fails to provide this basic form of equality, Kant's criticism of morganatic marriage does not entail a rejection of all forms of inequalities (especially natural inequalities) within the household, as made clear in MM 6: 279. I tend to agree with Pascoe's reading (cf. Pascoe 2018, 19–21).

and the equality it entails were notions of special interest to jurists and feminist scholars in his day. In weighing in on these issues, Kant's account of marriage is not especially innovative. Rather, it innovates by committing more explicitly to the equality of spouses in marriage, by properly acknowledging the political power held by marriage in society, and by taking seriously the consequences of not being able to enter that institution. It also carries important limitations: unlike feminist writers in his day, Kant does not question broader social and political inequalities that are at risk of compromising the equality he wishes to secure within marriage.

But Kant's conception of marriage also raises questions that feminist perspectives on marriage, from the eighteenth century to the present, have sought to address – such as how marriage may be able to address threats of sexual objectification, how a legal institution like marriage can ensure equal rights and protections for spouses, and what kind of reforms may be necessary to gender equality in (but also beyond) marriage. Kant's account of marriage proves to be helpful in navigating these questions, and Kant's philosophy of right, despite certain limitations, seems capable of supporting more egalitarian goals than those he set forth. But these transformative possibilities still unfold against the backdrop of the exclusion of those who are not able to enter marriage. While Kant expresses displeasure at those who are wealthy enough to marry but choose to remain single – as he regards them as partly responsible for the existence of abandoned children (MM 6: 326–327) –, many others were not single by choice. While Kant did not even envision same-sex marriage as an option, he was aware that many working-class men and women did not meet the legal requirements to marry or were unable to afford it.[80] While marriage may be able to significantly improve the lives of those who enter it, this leaves us struggling with the question of those who can't – and wondering if marriage can ever be a truly inclusive institution, given how much gatekeeping it has consistently generated. This perhaps marks the limits of my own investigation, and points to those of others. Pascoe, for instance, argues that marriage is bound to be discriminatory: even when some sexualities get decriminalized, marriage is still used to reinforce the legitimacy of the state-sanctioned sexualities at the expense of others (Pascoe 2018, 18). Alternatively, Brake has proposed a nondiscriminatory account of marriage ("minimal marriage") motivated by the assumption that liberal justice must be able to provide a legal framework supporting the caring relationships at the core of marriage (Brake 2012). In investigating Kant's account of marriage

---

[80] It is widely known that Kant disapproved of the marriage of his servant Martin Lampe and of the "additional expense" that created for him (Kuehn 2001, 223). Kuehn notes, though, that Kant did not hold a grudge against Lampe ... as he ended up benefitting from the domestic labour accomplished by Lampe's family (Kuehn 2001, 477 n133).

and the transformative possibilities it carries, I do not have the pretension to settle the question of whether the existence of marriage is a good thing or not – but I hope to have shown that as an institution that is unlikely to go anywhere, it carries interesting transformative possibilities for Kantian philosophy and its interlocutors. Acknowledging the limitations of Kant's account of marriage is an important part of that investigation, and points to the necessity of the criticisms and changes that have contributed to making marriage a much more inclusive institution today than in eighteenth-century Germany, starting with the social reforms that Kant himself was not eager to embrace.[81] It also allows us to make room for voices like those of Hippel or Ehrmann who have not had Kant's luck in becoming part of the philosophical canon, but still offer valuable reflections on marriage that may have contributed to shaping Kant's views – and that reflect rich and complex conceptions of gender equality of their own.

---

[81] This is in no way implying that marriage does not carry its fair share of problems today – but I do think we have made progress. Despite a climate of increasing political polarization and intolerance, I am confident that many of us will keep fighting for an equal access to marriage for those who wish to enter it – and also, importantly, for truly equal opportunities for those who prefer not to, or who wish to leave that institution.

References

Achenwall, Gottfried. (2021) *Natural Law*. Edited by Pauline Kleingeld, (trans. Corinna Vermeulen). Bloomsbury Press.

Altman, Matthew. (2010) "Kant on Sex and Marriage: The Implications for the Same-Sex Marriage Debate." *Kant-Studien* 101 (3), 309–330.

Baier, Annette. (1993) "Moralism and Cruelty: Reflections on Hume and Kant." *Ethics* 103 (3), 436–457.

Beever, Allan. (2013) "Kant on the Law of Marriage." *Kantian Review* 18 (3), 339–362.

Biester, Johann Erich. (1783) "Vorschlag, die Geistlichen nicht mehr bei Vollziehung der Ehen zu bemühen." *Berlinische Monatsschrift* 2, 265–276.

Bock, Gisela, & Zimmermann, Margarete. (1997) "Die *Querelle des Femmes* in Europa." In Gisela Bock, Margarete Zimmermann, & Monika Kopyczinski (eds.), Quer*elles*. J. B. Metzler.

Brake, Elizabeth. (2005) "Justice and Virtue in Kant's Account of Marriage." *Kantian Review* 9, 58–94.

(2012) *Minimizing Marriage: Marriage, Morality, and the Law*. Oxford University Press.

Brandt, Reinhard. (1999) "Kants Forderung der Todesstrafe bei Duell- und Kindesmord". In Peter Niesen and Hauke Brunkhorst (eds.) *Das Recht der Republik*. Suhrkamp, 268–287.

Broad, Jacqueline. (2014) "Mary Astell on Marriage and Lockean Slavery." *History of Political Thought* 35 (4), 717–738.

Campt, Tina M. (2003) "Converging Spectres of an Other within: Race and Gender in Prewar Afro-German History". *Callaloo* 26 (2), 322–341.

Dyck, Corey W. (2021) "Introduction". In Corey W. Dyck (ed.), *Women and Philosophy in Eighteenth-Century Germany*. Oxford University Press, 1–7.

Dawson, Ruth. (1986) "'And This Shield Is Called – Self-Reliance'. Emerging Feminist Consciousness in the Late Eighteenth Century." In Ruth-Ellen Joeres & Mary Jo Maynes (eds.), *German Women in the Eighteenth and Nineteenth Centuries*. Indiana University Press, 157–174.

Deligiorgi, Katerina. (2005) *Kant and the Culture of Enlightenment*. SUNY Press.

Denis, Lara. (1999) "Kant on the Wrongness of 'Unnatural' Sex". *History of Philosophy Quarterly* 16 (2), 225–248.

References

Denis, Lara. (2001) "From Friendship to Marriage: Revising Kant." *Philosophy and Phenomenological Research* 63 (1), 1–28.

Donahue, Charles. (2016) "The Legal Background: European Marriage Law from 16th to 19th century." In Silvana Menchi (ed.), *Marriage in Europe, 1400–1800*. University of Toronto Press, 33–60.

Du Moulin, Charles. (1546) *Tractatus commerciorum et usurarum, redituumque pecunia constitutorum et monetarum*. Galliot Du Pré.

Dworkin, Andrea. (1974) *Woman Hating: A Radical Look at Sexuality*. E. P. Dutton.

Ehrmann, Marianne. (1790) *Die unglückliche Hanne*. Projekt Gutenberg. [www.projekt-gutenberg.org/ehrmann/unghanne/unghanne.html]

Emmett, Kelin. (2022) "Resisting Marriage, Reclaiming Right: An (Early) Modern Critique of Marriage." *Journal of the American Philosophical Association* 8 (4), 721–740.

Eser, Albin. (1986) "Reform of German Abortion Law: First Experiences". *The American Journal of Comparative Law* 34 (2), 369–383.

Firestone, Shulamith. (1970) *The Dialectic of Sex: The Case for Feminist Revolution*. Morrow.

Fleischacker, Samuel. (2013) *What Is Enlightenment?* Routledge.

Forbes, Allauren. (2019) "Mary Astell on Bad Custom and Epistemic Injustice." *Hypatia* 34 (4), 777–801.

Fronius, Helen. (2003) *The Diligent Dilettante: Women Writers in Germany 1770–1820*. University of Oxford. [https://ora.ox.ac.uk/objects/uuid:d95009fe-e8ea-4bcf-b520-29f2e9e849b5/download_file?file_format=application%2Fpdf&safe_filename=602323289.pdf&type_of_work=Thesis]

Garcia, Manon. (2023) *The Joy of Consent: A Philosophy of Good Sex*. Harvard University Press.

Gerlings, Jonas. (2017) *Freedom in Conflict: On Kant's Critique of Medical Reason*. European University Institute. PhD Thesis. [https://hdl.handle.net/1814/45887]

Goyard-Fabre, Simone. (1996) *La Philosophie du droit de Kant*. J. Vrin.

Guyer, Paul. (2000) *Kant on Freedom, Law, and Happiness*. Cambridge University Press.

Herman, Barbara. (1993) "Could It Be Worth Thinking about Kant on Sex and Marriage?" In Louise M. Antony & Charlotte Witt (eds.), *A Mind of One's Own: Feminist Essays on Reason and Objectivity*. Westview Press, 49–68.

Hull, Isabel. (1996) *Sexuality, State, and Civil Society in Germany, 1700–1815*. Cornell University Press.

Kant, Immanuel. (1996) *The Metaphysics of Morals* (trans. M. Gregor). Cambridge University Press.

References

(1997) *Critique of Practical Reason* (trans. M. Gregor). Cambridge University Press.

(1997) *Lectures on Ethics* (trans. P. Heath & J. B. Schneewind). Cambridge University Press.

(1998) *Critique of Pure Reason* (trans. P. Guyer & A. Wood). Cambridge University Press.

(2006) *Anthropology from a Pragmatic Point of View* (trans. R. Louden). Cambridge University Press.

(2006) "Idea for a Universal History from a Cosmopolitan Perspective." In Pauline Kleingeld (ed.), *Toward Perpetual Peace and Other Writings on Politics, Peace, and History*. Yale University Press, 3–16.

(2006) "An Answer to the Question: What Is Enlightenment." In Pauline Kleingeld, (ed.), *Toward Perpetual Peace and Other Writings on Politics, Peace, and History*. Yale University Press, 17–23.

(2006) "On the Common Saying: This May Be True in Theory, but It Does Not Hold in Practice." In Pauline Kleingeld (ed.), *Toward Perpetual Peace and Other Writings on Politics, Peace, and History*. Yale University Press, 44–66.

(2012) *Groundwork of the Metaphysics of Morals* (trans. M. J. Gregor & J. Timmermann). Cambridge University Press.

Kleingeld, Pauline. (2019) "On Dealing with Kant's Sexism and Racism." *SGIR Review* 2 (2), 3–22.

Korsgaard, Christine. (1996) *Creating the Kingdom of Ends*. Cambridge University Press.

Kuehn, Manfred. (2001) *Kant: A Biography*. Cambridge University Press.

Kundert, Ursula (2003). "The Polemic Trap: German Querelle Des Femmes and Misogynous Satire in the 17th Century." *Intellectual News* 11 (1), 57–63.

Lewis, Margaret Brannan. (2016) *Infanticide and Abortion in Early Modern Germany*. Routledge.

Louden, Robert. (2021) "A Mere Skeleton of the Sciences? Amalia Holst's Critique of Basedow and Campe." In Corey W. Dyck (ed.), *Women and Philosophy in Eighteenth-Century Germany*. Oxford University Press, 72–92.

Madland, Helga. (1989) "Infanticide as Fiction: Goethe's Urfaust and Schiller's 'Kindsmörderin' as Models." *The German Quarterly* 62 (1), 27–38.

(1992) "Gender and the German Literary Canon: Marianne Ehrmann's Infanticide Fiction." *Monatshefte* 84 (4), 405–416.

Mertens, Thomas. (2014) "Sexual Desire and the Importance of Marriage in Kant's Philosophy of Law." *Ratio Juris* 27 (3), 330–343.

Michalik, Kerstin. (2006) "The Development of the Discourse on Infanticide in the Late Eighteenth Century and the New Legal Standardization of the Offense in the Nineteenth Century." In Marion Gray & Ulrike Gleixner (eds.), *Gender in Transition: Discourse and Practice in German-Speaking Europe, 1750–1830*. University of Michigan Press, 51–71.

Moses, Julia. (2019) "From Faith to Race? 'Mixed Marriage' and the Politics of Difference in Imperial Germany." *The History of the Family* 24 (3), 466–493.

Okin, Susan Moller. (1982) "Women and the Making of the Sentimental Family." *Philosophy & Public Affairs* 11 (1), 65–88.

O'Neill, Eileen & Lascano, Marcy. (2019) *Feminist History of Philosophy: The Recovery and Evaluation of Women's Philosophical Thought*. Springer.

Papadaki, Evangelia. (2007) "Sexual Objectification: From Kant to Contemporary Feminism." *Contemporary Political Theory* 6 (3), 330–348.

(2010) "Kantian Marriage and Beyond: Why It Is Worth Thinking about Kant on Marriage." *Hypatia* 25 (2), 276–294.

Pascoe (2011). "Personhood, Protection, and Promiscuity: Kant on Infanticide and Institutions." Unpublished draft. [https://jordanpascoe.wordpress.com/wp-content/uploads/2012/02/pascoeinfanticide.pdf]

(2018) "A Universal Estate: On Kant and Marriage Equality." In Larry Krasnoff, Nuria Sánchez Madrid, & Paula Satne (eds.), *Kant's Doctrine of Right in the 21st Century*. University of Wales Press, 220–240.

(2019) "On Finding Yourself in a State of Nature: A Kantian Account of Abortion and Voluntary Motherhood." *Feminist Philosophy Quarterly* 5 (3), 1–28.

(2022) *Kant's Theory of Labour*. Cambridge University Press.

Pateman, Carole. (1988) *The Sexual Contract*. Stanford University Press.

Piché, Claude. (2012) "Kant et l'esprit de secte en philosophie." In Stefano Bacin, Alfredo Ferrarin, Claudio La Rocca & Margit Ruffing (eds.), *Kant und die Philosophie in Weltbürgerlicher Absicht, Akten des XI. Internationalen Kant Kongresses*, De Gruyter, 691–702.

(2015) "Kantian Enlightenment as a Critique of Culture." *Con-Textos Kantianos* 2 (2), 197–216.

Rich, Adrienne. (1995) *Of Woman Born: Motherhood as Experience and Institution*. Norton.

Sabourin, Charlotte. (2021a) "Kant's Enlightenment and Women's Peculiar Immaturity." *Kantian Review* 26 (2), 235–260.

(2021b) "Theodor von Hippel on the Status of Women in Germany." In Corey W. Dyck (ed.), *Women and Philosophy in Eighteenth-Century Germany*. Oxford University Press, 157–178.

(2023a) "'Nature and Society Give Women a Great Habit of Suffering': Germaine de Staël's Feminism and Its Challenges." *Southern Journal of Philosophy* 61 (1), 133–157.

(2023b) "Critical Perspectives on Religion." In Karen Detlefsen & Lisa Shapiro (eds.), *The Routledge Handbook of Women and Early Modern European Philosophy*. Routledge, 337–349.

Schmidt, James. (1989) "The Question of Enlightenment: Kant, Mendelssohn, and the Mittwochsgesellschaft." *Journal of the History of Ideas* 50 (2), 269–291.

Sticker, Martin. (2020) "The Case against Different-Sex Marriage in Kant." *Kantian Review* 25 (3), 441–464.

Stuckenberg, Johann Heinrich Willbrand (1882) *The Life of Immanuel Kant*. Thoemmes Press.

Sussman, David. (2008) "Shame and Punishment in Kant's 'Doctrine of Right'." *The Philosophical Quarterly* 231 (58), 299–317.

Timmermann, Jens. (2022) "The Quandary of Infanticide in Kant's 'Doctrine of Right'." *Archiv für Geschichte der Philosophie* 106 (2), 267–294.

Uleman, Jennifer. (2000) "On Kant, Infanticide, and Finding Oneself in a State of Nature." *Zeitschrift für philosophische Forschung* 54 (2), 173–195.

Varden, Helga. (2017) "Kant and Women." *Pacific Philosophical Quarterly* 98 (4), 653–694.

(2020) *Sex, Love, and Gender: A Kantian Theory*. Oxford University Press.

von Berlepsch, Emilie. (1791) "Ueber einige zum Glück der Ehe nothwendige Eigenschaften und Grundsätze." *Neuer Teutscher Merkur* 2, 63–102.

von Hippel, Theodor Gottlieb (2009) *The Status of Women: Collected Writings*. Edited by Timothy F. Sellner. Xlibris.

Westphal, Kenneth R. (1997) "Do Kant's Principles Justify Property or Usufruct?" *Jahrbuch für Recht und Ethik* 5, 141–194.

Williams, Howard. (1983) *Kant's Political Philosophy*. Basil Blackwell.

(2006) "Liberty, Equality, and Independence: Core Concepts in Kant's Political Philosophy." In Graham Bird (ed.), *A Companion to Kant*. Blackwell Books, 364–383.

Wilson, Donald. (2004) "Kant and the Marriage Right." *Pacific Philosophical Quarterly* 85 (1), 103–123.

Wolff, Christian. (1747) *Vernünfftige Gedancken Von dem Gesellschafftlichen Leben der Menschen Und insonderheit Dem gemeinen Wesen: Zu Beförderung der Glückseeligkeit des menschlichen Geschlechtes*. Renger.

Wood, Allen W. (1999) *Kant's Ethical Thought*. Cambridge University Press.
  (2008) *Kantian Ethics*. Cambridge University Press.
Wunder, Heide. (2016) "Marriage in the Holy Roman Empire of the German Nation." In Silvana Menchi (ed.), *Marriage in Europe, 1400–1800*. University of Toronto Press, 61–93.

Acknowledgements

I would like to thank Howard Williams and two anonymous referees for their thorough and useful feedback on earlier drafts of this Element. I have also shared parts of this work with various publics, all of which contributed to its development. I am especially grateful to Emily Carson, Marguerite Deslauriers, and Barbara Herman, who commented on my first reflections on this topic. Many thanks to my writing group colleagues Allauren, Louise, Michaela, Michaela, and Simona for their helpful suggestions and support. Finally, I owe special thanks to Jason Voss for his unconditional support (writing on marriage is much easier with a good partner), and to my family and friends for their encouragement.

Acknowledgements

Cambridge Elements⹀

The Philosophy of Immanuel Kant

Desmond Hogan
Princeton University

Desmond Hogan joined the philosophy department at Princeton in 2004. His interests include Kant, Leibniz and German rationalism, early modern philosophy, and questions about causation and freedom. Recent work includes 'Kant on the Foreknowledge of Contingent Truths', *Res Philosophica* 91(1) (2014); 'Kant's Theory of Divine and Secondary Causation', in Brandon Look (ed.) *Leibniz and Kant*, Oxford University Press (2021); 'Kant and the Character of Mathematical Inference', in Carl Posy and Ofra Rechter (eds.) *Kant's Philosophy of Mathematics Vol. I*, Cambridge University Press (2020).

Howard Williams
University of Cardiff

Howard Williams was appointed Honorary Distinguished Professor at the Department of Politics and International Relations, University of Cardiff in 2014. He is also Emeritus Professor in Political Theory at the Department of International Politics, Aberystwyth University, a member of the Coleg Cymraeg Cenedlaethol (Welsh-language national college) and a Fellow of the Learned Society of Wales. He is the author of *Marx* (1980); *Kant's Political Philosophy* (1983); *Concepts of Ideology* (1988); *Hegel, Heraclitus and Marx's Dialectic* (1989); *International Relations in Political Theory* (1992); *International Relations and the Limits of Political Theory* (1996); *Kant's Critique of Hobbes: Sovereignty and Cosmopolitanism* (2003); *Kant and the End of War* (2012) and is currently editor of the journal Kantian Review. He is writing a book on the Kantian legacy in political philosophy for a new series edited by Paul Guyer.

Allen Wood
Indiana University

Allen Wood is Ward W. and Priscilla B. Woods Professor Emeritus at Stanford University. He was a John S. Guggenheim Fellow at the Free University in Berlin, a National Endowment for the Humanities Fellow at the University of Bonn and Isaiah Berlin Visiting Professor at the University of Oxford. He is on the editorial board of eight philosophy journals, five book series and The Stanford Encyclopedia of Philosophy. Along with Paul Guyer, Professor Wood is co-editor of The Cambridge Edition of the Works of Immanuel Kant and translator of the Critique of Pure Reason. He is the author or editor of a number of other works, mainly on Kant, Hegel and Karl Marx. His most recently published books are *Fichte's Ethical Thought*, Oxford University Press (2016) and *Kant and Religion*, Cambridge University Press (2020). Wood is a member of the American Academy of Arts and Sciences.

About the Series

This Cambridge Elements series provides an extensive overview of Kant's philosophy and its impact upon philosophy and philosophers. Distinguished Kant specialists provide an up-to-date summary of the results of current research in their fields and give their own take on what they believe are the most significant debates influencing research, drawing original conclusions.

Cambridge Elements

The Philosophy of Immanuel Kant

Elements in the Series

The Kantian Federation
Luigi Caranti

The Politics of Beauty: A Study of Kant's Critique of Taste
Susan Meld Shell

Kant's Theory of Labour
Jordan Pascoe

Kant's Late Philosophy of Nature: The Opus postumum
Stephen Howard

Kant on Freedom
Owen Ware

Kant on Self-Control
Marijana Vujošević

Kant on Rational Sympathy
Benjamin Vilhauer

The Moral Foundation of Right
Paul Guyer

The Postulate of Public Right
Patrick Capps and Julian Rivers

Kant on the History and Development of Practical Reason
Olga Lenczewska

Kant's Ideas of Reason
Katharina T. Kraus

Kant on Marriage
Charlotte Sabourin

A full series listing is available at: www.cambridge.org/EPIK

For EU product safety concerns, contact us at Calle de José Abascal, 56–1°, 28003 Madrid, Spain or eugpsr@cambridge.org.

www.ingramcontent.com/pod-product-compliance
Ingram Content Group UK Ltd.
Pitfield, Milton Keynes, MK11 3LW, UK
UKHW022035300325
456910UK00008B/45